PRAISE FOR

ONE BAD MOTHER

Best Memoir 2024 Finalist, Pacific Book Awards

"Real. Raw. Laugh out loud funny—like motherhood itself. In *One Bad Mother*, Megan Williams makes us all feel like good mothers, doing the best we can while on the craziest adventure of our lives."

—Leslie Morgan Steiner, author of *Crazy Love, Mommy Wars, The Naked Truth,* and *The Baby Chase*

· · · · ·

"In *One Bad Mother*, Megan Williams takes us on a riveting, unvarnished journey as she navigates the complexities of motherhood and the rigorous demands of police training. Her narrative is both heartbreaking and inspiring, shedding light on the unseen sacrifices and triumphs that come with redefining your identity. Megan's honesty and vulnerability make this a deeply relatable and inspirational read. Her story is also a powerful testament to the inner strength that lies within every woman."

—Natalie MacLean, author of *Wine Witch on Fire: Rising from the Ashes of Divorce, Defamation, and Drinking Too Much*

· · · · ·

"*One Bad Mother* by Megan Williams is an engaging, emotionally resonant portrayal of a woman seeking validation as a new mother, a role that has upturned her identity. Williams examines motherhood, with all its joys and pressures, amid a culture that too often mutes discussion of the staggering societal expectations all mothers face. An entertaining, refreshing read!"

—Kristin Beck, author of *Courage, My Love* and *The Winter Orphans*

"Former competitive runner, literature professor, and self-described harsh grader, most notably of herself, Megan Williams meets her match with the birth of preemie twins. Suddenly, all the things she's trained for and is good at are not the skills she needs to survive this grueling, mid-life passage. Then a chance meeting on a Philadelphia track puts her on the path to becoming a police officer.

In *One Bad Mother: A Mother's Search for Meaning in the Police Academy,* Williams skillfully weaves together her twin ordeals—to keep her children alive and thriving, and also join one of the largest, toughest police departments in the country.

Smartly written and laced with dark humor, *One Bad Mother* is a powerful story that will resonate with anyone who questions cultural norms and how they shape our expectations. It's for anyone who wonders who they've become at mid-life and fears they've lost their way. Deftly layered with references to the literature she loves, Williams discovers sometimes the biggest test we have to pass in life is not the one we set out to take. A riveting, fast-paced read."

—Carol Smith, author of *Crossing the River: Seven Stories That Saved My Life, a Memoir*

• • • • •

"*One Bad Mother* is a ride into the familiar and the unknown, making this memoir both relatable and fascinating. Tapping into cultural expectations, and the lives of women, Williams explores what it means to be a mother fielding opportunities, facing limits and making choices."

—Corie Adjmi, author of *The Marriage Box*

• • • • •

"*One Bad Mother* is a fearless, honest, and, at times, humorous peek into the challenges of modern motherhood and how we cope when there's a disconnect between reality and our dreams."

—Lisa Cooper Ellison, author, speaker, and trauma-informed writing coach

ONE BAD MOTHER

A Mother's Search *for* Meaning *in the* Police Academy

MEGAN WILLIAMS

Sibylline
PRESS

AN IMPRINT OF ALL THINGS BOOK

Published in the United States by Sibylline Press,
an imprint of All Things Book LLC, California.
Sibylline Press is dedicated to publishing the brilliant work
of women authors ages 50 and older.
www.sibyllinepress.com

Distributed to the trade by Publishers Group West.
Sibylline Press
Paperback ISBN: 9781960573858
eBook ISBN: 9781960573131
Library of Congress Control Number: 2024934182

Book and Cover Design: Alicia Feltman

This book pulls significantly from the past. As a memoir, the ever-changing and subjective nature of individual memory structures the narrative. To the best of my ability, I have recreated the past based on my notes. Whenever possible, names have been changed to protect an individual's privacy. In some instances, places and sicknesses have also been substituted to make them less identifiable.

Portions of *One Bad Mother* have received recognition from the New Millennium Award in Nonfiction, the Cagibi Magazine Prize, Panther Creek Award in Non-Fiction, and William Faulkner Creative Writers' Competition. In 2023, Williams won the Pacific Northwest Writers Association (PNWA) award for nonfiction.

ONE BAD MOTHER

A Mother's Search *for* Meaning
in the Police Academy

MEGAN WILLIAMS

Always and forever to Gus and Grace.

"To infinity and beyond."
—Buzz Lightyear

TABLE OF CONTENTS

INTRODUCTION

NOVEMBER 2023
BELLINGHAM, WA

test *noun*

1. An examination of somebody's knowledge or ability, consisting of questions for them to answer or activities for them to perform; 2. A medical examination to discover what is wrong with you or to check the condition of your health; 3. An experiment to discover whether or how well something works, or to find out more information about it; 4. A situation or an event that shows how good, strong, etc. somebody/something is (*Oxford English Dictionary*).

BY THE TIME A PERSON HAS REACHED THE AGE OF FORTY-FIVE, as I had when I applied to the police academy, she's taken more tests than she can count. Some blend together, an endless procession of graphite circles. The SATs, the GREs, the APs. I cannot recall a single question from these tests, just the cramping of my right hand and the background whir of a pencil sharpener. Some tests resurface as nightmares, where I dream and fail, again and again. Psychologists call this imposter syndrome, a benign term that does not approximate the sleeping terror that comes when I flunk high school English, my subsequent life as a teacher exposed as a fraud. Some tests I cannot forget. The score of 52 I received on my first college chemistry exam. The teacher's note scrawled inside my blue book: *Please see me, ASAP*. For the rest of the semester's tests, I sat, paralyzed, breathing the cloying smell of formaldehyde, my hand shaking so badly I couldn't hold the pencil.

In life, there are tests you fail, tests for which you are over-prepared, tests that no one passes, tests that are graded on a curve, tests that you can retake. Some tests—like a drug or a pregnancy test—have only one right answer. When I was doing hormone treatment to get pregnant, the nurse warned me not to take a pregnancy test. It would show a false positive. After two years of trying, two years of failed tests, I ignored her and peed on the stick. I just wanted to see those two blue lines, to imagine a simpler life, one that didn't involve putting my eggs in a petri dish.

Sometimes in life we can test the waters, comfortable in the belief that we can retreat if the outcome is unpleasant, just as we can dip a toe in a too-cold lake. But when we test the waters, we ignore the fact that some tests are final. No retreat to a warm lounge chair in the sun. No undo. No re-do. We pass, or we fail.

"Why is this science test so hard?" my children complain. They are high schoolers in a world where every test can be retaken and everyone gets a participation award.

"Do you want a life filled with easy tests?" I ask.

"Yes," they say.

Each year when I was in middle school, we took the Lincoln Spelling Test, a hundred words that were each read in separate sentences by the teacher. We were supposed to transcribe the word perfectly into a four-page booklet. Passing grade was seventy percent. As the words became incrementally more difficult, my classmates wrote in rounded cursive, while I stumbled and stuttered. By the fifteenth word, rubber eraser crumbs covered my page. Every year I failed, and every year I was stuck inside at recess with my corrections. I knew the meanings of the words, but they got caught and jumbled when I tried to sound them out. Even then, I wanted more than anything to write—poems, stories, maybe even a book. *Achieve. Definitely. Gauge.* Without spelling these words, I had no future as a writer.

Looking back at a life filled with tests, I can see that the most difficult ones were the ones I assigned myself—the 3:10 marathon time (fail). The PhD in English (pass). Ironman Lake Placid (pass). I was a harsh grader. My own worst critic. These tests had only one right answer: I had to win. Being the fastest or getting the highest grade was the only metric that told me I was good enough.

In December of 2014, I began the application process for the Philadelphia Police Academy. The admissions tests were endless: the Nelson-Denny reading test, the physical fitness test, the Personal Data Questionnaire, the background check and interview, the drug test(s) and physical, the polygraph, the Minnesota Multiphasic Personality Inventory Test (MMPI), the psychiatric evaluation, and the Chain of Command evaluation. These tests swallowed two plus years of my life—all just to make it to day one of the academy, where the commissioner told ninety candidates we had passed "the ultimate test."

Before the first day at the academy, if asked, I would have said that the ultimate test of my life was motherhood. Creating two human beings from scratch. Breastfeeding twins. Maybe something as seemingly mundane as trying to spoon organic squash into a turtle-loving toddler who spent mealtimes with her head retracted inside her shirt. In the predominantly male academy, motherhood was the furthest thing from a test; it was an aside, an inconvenience that made candidates late—or a gift to be wrapped in saccharine rhetoric about protecting the unborn "innocents."

On day one, the police recruits were the "lucky" ones. The Fortunate Few. We had "made it." We had passed all the tests.

"For every one of you sitting there," the commissioner said, "there are fifteen people who failed, who wanted to be here but couldn't cut it." Assuming that the commissioner wasn't exaggerating, with a 6.25 percent acceptance rate, it was as difficult to get into the Philadelphia Police Academy as it was to be admitted to Princeton (6 percent) or Yale (7 percent).

When I was admitted into the academy, I still didn't understand the purpose of these tests—whether the department was trying to weed out the bad candidates or admit the good. There is a difference. At each milestone, the department re-emphasized the possibility of failure, and I, being a type-A competitive person, refocused my goals. I became so caught up in the hope of advancing, I forgot the purpose of the journey. The academy admission process focused on tangibles—blood tests, hearing tests, running times—avoiding the subjective part of "test," the part that measures how "good" or "strong" someone is. While the tests were based in concrete metrics, the rhetoric surrounding them was not; if we passed, we could "be the difference," standing proudly together in our shiny dress uniforms. The sheer number of tests suggested a complete dispersal of responsibility, the refusal of any single person or entity to be held accountable for admitting a candidate—to the point where the department relied on the polygraph, a test considered so fallible and obsolete it is no longer admissible in courtrooms.

Throughout the recruitment process, ethical questions were just another metric, with a single desired answer. In my background interview, my psychological evaluation, and the MMPI, I was asked what I would do if I saw a superior officer steal a bottle of water from a neighborhood store. I studied for these tests. I knew the "correct" answer. So I responded: *file a report against the superior officer*. In other words, I lied. Maybe this was cheating. Maybe, in a life filled with "achievement" tests, I had simply learned how to "take the test." Whatever it was, as a metric, these sorts of questions and ethical tests slowly strip away your humanity if the answer, each and every time, is not to make a decision, but to defer to a higher authority. Maybe that is the whole point. Needless to say, I passed this question—all three times it was posed. But I also knew that in real life, if I had a partner who stole a bottle of water, I would either confront that person or ignore the incident completely. Life is too short to create a crisis over a bottle of Poland Springs. Society's focus on tests forgets that there are no definitive tests for the most important things in life—being a good person, partner, or parent. Maybe there is no test for what makes a good police officer. But, as I learned in my two years applying to the PPD, if you focus on the tests, you distract yourself just long enough from evaluating how well you are doing in your personal present. You fool yourself into believing that if you complete the next challenge, if you jump the next hurdle the department puts in front of you, you will become extraordinary.

CHAPTER ONE

SETTING THE BAR

NOVEMBER 2015
PHILADELPHIA POLICE TRAINING FACILITY

THE POLICE ACADEMY SQUATTED LIKE AN AIRPORT TERMINAL between the endless blocks of twin houses that made up Northeast Philadelphia. A buffer zone of cement and razor wire separated the campus from its suburban neighborhood. As I drove down those streets for the first time, window shades rose to a dreary Saturday. Blue-collar boots shuffled to work, slippered feet padded down front walks for newspapers. Inside the hallways of the Police Training Center, we, the candidates, had done something wrong before we even arrived. Officers clogged the hall. Slouched together, some with one leg of their baggy pants propped against a wall, they waited, watching, berating us as we funneled through the front door to run the gauntlet. *Honor. Integrity. Service*, the recruiting pamphlet promised. Here, candidates had the chance to be something extraordinary, should we be lucky and talented enough to pass the admission tests. Police officers got to "Be. The. Difference." We were poised to be part of a collective, something larger, something more concrete—something completely different from my stay-at-home life, where all I did was fail the test that was motherhood.

"State your age when you stand on the scale," a push from behind said. The woman in front of me scooted off the scale and into another room. "Not that way." She backtracked and stuttered "sorry."

Confused by the yelling, I waved my identification card. "Number 553," I announced, adding a faint "please?"

"We don't care about your number. Get on the scale." I bent to pull my shoes off.

"Keep those on," a voice behind me directed. I stepped up.

"One hundred and thirty-nine pounds," another voice recorded.

"Age!" the voice barked.

"Forty-five."

Officers ushered me down the hallway and into a packed classroom. I was the last of the forty-three recruits to arrive. Metal chairs scraped across the linoleum floor and recruits shifted nervously. There were rows of crewcut heads, a few women, maybe a handful of people my age. This was a familiar room—perfect, in its dullness, for standardized testing—nondescript desks, perfunctorily erased blackboards, industrial chairs with felt pads on their feet, gunked with dust.

A large man parked himself in front of us, legs splayed, two hands cupping his gun. "I'm Detective MacDonald. I work in the Background Investigative Unit." So far, I'd counted thirty firearms. The idea that someday soon I might stop counting depressed me. "I do the background interviews." MacDonald puffed out his chest. "Let me give you a few pieces of advice." He opened his hand to count and teetered. A seventies commercial surfaced in my consciousness. Weebles wobbled but they didn't fall down. "One: Do not wear sweats. The interview is business casual, which means nice pants and a shirt with a collar. Two: Wear deodorant." His face grim, he wasn't joking. "Three." He peeled a finger back, making us wait for the key point. "This is a big one. Don't smoke a doobie before your interview."

My teeth clamped down to stop the laughter, while my fellow recruits sat, mouths open like guppies, gulping down his advice.

Apparently, I was going to be the only one who tripped on the bar established by the police department because it was set so fucking low.

"Tell the truth and remember those three things," he flashed his fingers again, "and you'll be fine. Now, let's hustle downstairs to the gym."

I'd signed up to be a part of something extraordinary, but the academy benchmarks were laughably low. Recruits were expected to have a ninth-grade reading ability; to be in the top 70 percent of the general population in terms of fitness, which, to me, meant that three out of ten suspects escaped. Everything was age and gender-graded, as if crime would slow down for a forty-something housewife like me. A twenty-year-old man had to run eight-minute miles for the longer run. I had to run a ten-minute mile. As a competitive runner, there was no way to talk about marathon splits without sounding like an ass. On my fortieth birthday, I'd run a 7:19 mile. Twenty-six times. In a row. Five years later, the fact that I hadn't broken 3:10 still pissed me off.

"Take a number," a huge sergeant yelled. He was Popeye in the flesh, his forearms bursting from an otherwise scrawny build. In a strange mimicry of my running life, in a gym like any other, filled with testosterone and pre-race anxiety, I pinned a bib to my chest. Number 23. We shifted our feet on the cold cement floor for ten minutes while Popeye set up the bench press. Some officers delivered paperwork to him; most chain-smoked in the doorway. We waited some more. We'd been in the gym for thirty minutes, and all we'd done was fifty jumping jacks. Recruits whispered—muffled discussions about people who were back because they'd failed something: the run, the polygraph, the background interview.

A drill instructor leaned against the open door and pointed to my Boston Marathon finisher's shirt. "Did you run that?"

"Yes."

He nodded. "You look like a runner." Something wistful crossed his face. "I'm trying to qualify."

"Number twenty-three," Popeye shouted.

"Here," I scooted forward.

"I've called your number three times." Red crept up his neck. "Did I not tell you not to talk?" Drowning in his double negatives, I said nothing. He stepped toward me. "If you can't take basic instruction," he said, throwing his words at me in a staccato rhythm, "then you need to consider another career choice."

I said nothing.

"Recruit, do you understand me?"

"Yes, sir."

"Harsh," a woman next to me whispered. I shrugged. If the police department thought they could break me with shouting, they were mistaken. I was a mom. All my kids did was yell at me. Motherhood was like trying to rationalize with someone on a bad acid trip. My seven-year-old twins Gus and Grace threw shoes at my head when I refused to stop at McDonald's.

The night before the academy test, a screech not unlike the keening of a fox woke me. Sliding straight down Gus's voice into panic mode, I shot out of bed while my husband Augie rubbed the sleep from his eyes, expecting the worst. The worst was bad. I never got to hold my children when they were born, eleven weeks early. Both babies were whisked away after an emergency C-section—passed through a window straight into the NICU. For the first three months at home, Gus would periodically turn blue during dinner. We'd thump his back because he was hypoxic and had forgotten how to breathe. This was just something preemie boys did. The NICU called them "Wimpy Whities" for a reason. They couldn't always remember the sequence of breathing and swallowing. Out of all the combinations of race and gender, the nurses joked, white boys were the last to leave the hospital. They knew a good thing when they had it.

I was the one to hear the scream in the night, to notice the flare of Gus's nostrils that indicated pneumonia. That was how it was. Even though they were now seven, their newborn cries were so firmly imprinted on me that I often woke to a phantom cry. Thinking they were in distress, I bolted into their rooms, only to be confronted by the visceral punch of memory. The children were fine, snuffling in sleep, their faces soft and drooly and healthy. These were no longer the crazy newborn days when they'd weighed two and half pounds each, when I'd believed, in my sleep-deprived state, that if I stayed awake, for just one more hour, I could protect them from SIDS.

I was Mom. I heard the screams in the night. At 3 a.m. the night before the academy test, Gus shrieked. He was sitting up in bed, hair matted in the way kids get because they are little night furnaces.

"Hi, Mom," he smiled, all dimples.

"Jesus Christ, Gus." I sat on his bed and felt his forehead. "What?"

"I just wanted some Oreos," he said, as if this made all the sense in the world.

"Um, what?" My eyes itched. "It's three in the morning."

"I'm hungry, Mommy," he explained patiently. "I want Oreos." And that was motherhood in a nutshell. Trying to rationalize with someone on a bad acid trip. Or getting yelled at the night before a test because your kid wanted Oreos at 3 a.m.

Back at the academy, a vacuum of silence followed Popeye's yelling. "Line up by age now," he directed. Thirty-five recruits remained. Six had failed the bench press, most of them women. A blonde woman with spiky hair behind me shook her arms.

"Nervous?" I asked her.

"Yeah. The shouting. This whole thing." She dipped her head, out of fear or disappointment, I couldn't tell.

"And we're the old ones," I said, loud enough so that everyone in my group heard.

"I'm Sam," the blonde stuck her hand out.

"Tricia," a middle-aged Black woman with a buzz cut announced. Compared to the sleek twenty-something military recruits ahead of us, we were a hodgepodge group, some squat, some tall, all of us pushing fifty.

"Sit-ups." Popeye ushered us to five stations. Somewhere in the neighborhood outside the gym, an aluminum door slammed, evidence of life.

"You first." A petite red-haired woman knelt on a mat and pointed to me. "Seventeen sit-ups in a minute. I hold your feet and time." I dropped, almost into her lap. My butt scooched closer to her and her chest pressed against my knees. She didn't smile, even though we were intimately locked together. "Go." Each time I rose, the sergeant and I were nose-to-nose, dogs circling each other cautiously. I hit seventeen. "Stop, stop." She released my feet.

"Can't I keep going?"

"No. It's pass/fail. Pass. Next."

Sam tapped my shoulder. "Nice job." The paramilitary atmosphere in the police academy was seductive. The curt commands and unsmiling faces of the officers had almost convinced me I was extraordinary. Then I remembered I had only done seventeen sit-ups in a minute. With someone holding my feet.

Listening to the chorus of "pass" and "fail," I wished the police department graded us. The concept of meritocracy governed my life. The faster I ran, the better my corral at the start of the Boston Marathon. The more I published, the more competitive I was for university jobs. On the police academy campus, faced with a system where I was praised for being mediocre; where there was always "good enough," I didn't know how to act.

The sit-up test decimated the group of twenty-something women. One by one, they disappeared, tails between their legs. Once again, everyone in my group passed.

"I guess when you get to be our age," I said as we returned to the start line for our final mile-and-a-half run, "you know how to prepare for anything. What do you guys do?"

"Do?"

"Yeah. As in work. You know, that thing when you aren't running around a crappy parking lot on a Saturday morning?"

"Ah, that." Sam laughed. "I'm a microbiologist."

"Of course you are. And I bet you have kids."

"A five-year-old."

"And you're just sick of your day job."

"Pretty much. You?"

"PhD in English. But mostly I'm a stay-at-home mom."

"So, you know."

"Yep, totally get it."

"I run a law office," Tricia said. "I had to train so hard for this run." She pulled her sweats from her legs, making a tent out of the weight she'd lost. "Never ran a day in my life. I lost thirty pounds." As much as I hated the shouting, the disorganization, and the waiting, my decision to apply to the academy felt right the minute I met those women. We were real; we were tough. We were prepared, and we were old.

Popeye led us to a large parking lot ringed by cones. We passed the huddle of sergeants, their cigarette smoke mixing with the cold air of an early winter. Now that the sun had risen, a kettledrum sky spread over us, overcast and implacable.

At the start line, the men elbowed their way to the front. "You all run together," Popeye declared. The military guys dwarfed me. This was going to be like the Ironman Lake Placid swim. Two thousand people converging on a single buoy. No wonder some women exited Mirror Lake with a black eye or a broken rib. Fill a man with race testosterone, and he'd run right over you. Every single time.

"What do you guys have to run?" I asked the men in front.

"Just under twelve minutes," a particularly brawny recruit bragged, his eyes focused behind me.

"You?" another recruit asked, bored.

"Sixteen minutes." My answer was mumbled, as if age were a personal weakness.

"Sixteen minutes?" Brawny said, checking out my legs. "I could crawl the time you have to run."

In an instant, it was on. Tricia, Sam, and I locked eyes. "Do it," Sam whispered. After waiting around for two hours, my legs were stiff as toothpicks. I'd planned to jog. Now, I was going to annihilate this guy, even if I had to cough up a lung to do it.

"Step forward to the line," Popeye pointed. "On your mark." I tensed forward. A recruit grabbed my shoulders and pushed me behind him.

"What the fuck?" I swore. The men laughed. My body filled with a familiar rage. *Underestimate me. That'll be fun.* Join the list, which started with Mrs. Hakes, my third-grade tutor who sounded out *"B" Is for Betsy* with me and told my parents I might never learn to read well.

Boarding school had made me a runner. In the fading light of another homesick afternoon, I ran. Thirteen and alone, three hundred miles from home, I ran, my only company the rotting apples on Orchard Hill and the lake, filled with swarms of dying mosquitoes. I ran because you cannot cry when you run. Pretty soon, sadness collided with adrenaline to become anger, which was so much easier to carry. Anger could be molded, grasped in each fist. It was concrete. Every person I passed became a victory.

"Get set. Go!" Popeye screamed. The crowd rushed away. No matter how many times I toed the start line, abandonment always hit me, as if a giant wave had crushed me and moved on, leaving me alone to tread water in the still air. There was one woman fifty meters ahead. She was out as if the start line were hot, legs pumping effortlessly. If she held this pace, there was no way I could catch her. I was a workhorse close to retirement. She was the real deal, a thoroughbred racing on her toes, leaning into the corners.

"Pretend you're fishing," I often told my running clients. "Pick someone ahead of you, cast your line, then reel them in." My hook landed on Brawny.

After the first lap, the fast woman put her hands on her hips and quit. An empty space, a momentary sadness, opened where she'd been. Two laps into the race, the men started to come back to me. I clawed my way to Brawny. By the third lap, we were shoulder-to-shoulder. He was panting. With a surge, I passed him. "Good job, buddy. You got this," I cheered, all sweetness and light, full of breath. He glowered and pumped his arms. I dropped him as if he were standing still, disappointed he didn't put up more of a fight.

As the laps passed, I felt good. My cadence high, I clicked off stride lengths. I wasn't running particularly fast, but compared to everyone else, I was an Olympian. Coming into the last lap, three guys were within striking distance. On the backstretch, I did something I'd never done before: I knew I could win, but I decided not to. Nothing at the academy that day had suggested that being the best would benefit me, either with the officers or with my fellow recruits. On the other side of the finish line, I deflated, the weight of not trying surprisingly heavy. The men peeled away without a word.

"Whew," Sam bent over. "I'm so happy that's over."

Tricia put her hands on her hips. "Girlfriend," she waved a finger at me, "you were flying."

"Remind me never to piss you off." Sam jumped back as if I'd punched her. Surrounded by a warm steam, we smiled our congratulations. At the end of the day, twenty-three recruits remained. Not a single old lady had been disqualified. That day, I had not yet learned that our combined age and experience came with a price, that I would be the only one of our group to make it into the academy.

Back in my car, the vents blew, hot as a dog's breath on my face. I dropped a shoulder out of my shirt and peeled my clammy jog bra over my waist. It was 12:30 p.m. and I was starving. An emptiness filled me, whether from the fitness test or from a rare Saturday morning away from my children, I didn't know. All I knew was that I was hungry and I wanted Oreos for lunch.

CHAPTER TWO

RUNNING IN CIRCLES

MY JOURNEY TO THE POLICE ACADEMY began thirteen months before the PE tests, on a high school track with a teen athlete named
Sarah. The scene was achingly familiar; maple leaves fell and rotted
in the still air, their syrupy smell the same as it had been during my
high school cross-country seasons, except that now I was the adult,
the coach, and a mother.

On the infield, a group of people waited at the 300-meter
mark, enjoying the last days of sun before our fall into darkness.
They were a hodgepodge of everything—all ages, heights, levels
of fitness. They weren't runners. There was too much cotton. Not
enough microfiber. Or gauntness. The men carried the heavy look
of CrossFit, their arms held away from their bodies, their lats huge,
as if they were jumbo jets, ready to lumber down the runway.

They high-fived one another while mumbling, "Nice work, nice
work." Some had walked the last 100 meters of their sprint. "You got it
anyway." A large man with a stopwatch stood at the finish line. "Walk
halfway around the track for the distance run," he told the group.

"Are you coming with us?" a man asked as I stepped onto the grass, waiting for Sarah to finish her warmup. I shook my head. He moved away, buoyed by the excitement of the others.

"What're you guys doing?" I asked the man with the stopwatch.

"Test for the police."

I kicked myself for not recognizing his close-clipped look, the officers on the sidelines, the white block letters spelling *Police Academy* across their broad shoulders.

I zeroed my watch for Sarah's next repeat. "Track, track!" I yelled as we came around the first turn, scattering the candidates. *Pain is relative,* I told myself as I swung onto the backstretch. Halfway around the track, my body felt used up, recycled. Caught between my failures as mother, writer, academic, and coach, I moved, but was directionless. White lines receded in front of me. I ran reluctantly, a Sisyphean hamster, doomed to repeat this one circle endlessly. Lost, I understood how I got here. Graduate school in English. Coaching to pay for the PhD. Marriage. Twins. What I didn't understand was where to go now, how to stop chasing after a sense of self rooted in physical pain and the need to be exceptional.

I wanted to believe I could begin again, that with each track repeat, I could reinvent myself. After years of teaching Fitzgerald's *The Great Gatsby,* I'd fallen in love with the idea of starting over. I wanted to become my own version of Gatsby, to spring from the Platonic conception of myself. My watch beeped. My splits were fast. I was running ahead of schedule. Sarah was behind me, but beating her gave me no sense of accomplishment. My life had grown stale. I was stagnating—facing middle age, refusing to believe I could no longer be anything or anyone I wanted. Deflated, another image surfaced. Me at twenty-two on a random Saturday evening in the musty stacks of Paley, the Temple University library. A first-year graduate student, I was scared, but energized by newness, by my potential to fail. This was the way I used to feel before every marathon. Before every class I taught or athlete I coached.

That's just nostalgia talking, I told myself as Sarah and I circled the track. *In your twenties, you smoked a pack a day and couldn't afford lettuce. You owned only black clothes. Your best friend was a cat.*

Sarah's footsteps quickened behind me, pulling me forward and away from the fact that my life was standing still, that the only path forward was determined by past choices.

"Go, go, go!" I screamed. Sarah drew even with me and exhaled. "No!" I yelled. "That's not good enough. Get. By. Me." She bolted the last fifty meters, her spikes throwing angry red rubber crumbs behind her. At the finish line, I swerved around her and patted her back.

"Nice work," I heaved. "Now, we do it again."

"I'm really tired." Her shoulders rose in mutiny.

"Look," I said, acknowledging that she was only thirteen. "Running hurts. You need to learn to distract yourself. Get a theme song. Something you turn on when the doubts start."

"What's yours?" she asked, flicking her ponytail across her shoulder like a metronome.

"My what?" It had been years since I'd interacted with a teenage girl. I'd forgotten how their conversations ran in tributaries, turning at a moment's notice.

"Your theme song?"

"Eminem's '*Business.*' Do you know it?" In the face of her silence, I sang, a forty-four-year-old mother out of breath from sprinting against an angry teenager: *I ain't got no time to play around. Is there a circus in town? Let's shut the shit down.*

"Isn't that song from like 2004?" Sarah asked. On the sidelines, her mother Nicky was pacing. I raised an eyebrow, and Nicky nodded.

"Sarah," I pointed to the start line. "Let's go again." After the next repeat, Sarah's sweaty hair stuck to her face. She stood, silhouetted against a blue sky pulled tight, and turned away. "Look," I tried to explain as we cooled down. "You have to breathe into that feeling. Accept it. Commit to the pain. Recognize that the doubts will always come. Accept them so you can move through them."

The air between us stilled. Affluent suburban homes backed up to the track, their yards dotted with pumpkins, their sides collapsing in the sun, and I wondered what I'd done wrong. After eight years of coaching high-school track and cross-country, I no longer took young clients. Their parents were too difficult. They complained that running was too hard, that I was too tough, then forgot to pick their kids up from practice. I'd made an exception for Sarah.

"She's had three heart surgeries," her mom Nicky told me when we first spoke. "For the first time in her life, she's been cleared to run. And running is all she wants to do." Our first session together had been fun, full of plyometric jumps and Sarah galloping colt-like across the infield.

"She needs to learn she no longer has limits," her mom explained. "She doesn't understand what normal pain feels like." At the time, Nicky's words had made sense. Now, as Sarah disintegrated with each lap, I wasn't so sure. Head hung low, she walked back to their car, the fabric of her shirt pulling tight across her training bra, and I realized I'd made a mistake. Between our first and second sessions, I'd forgotten that Sarah wasn't thirteen-year-old me, a sensitive lonely kid who learned to defend herself against the doubts by punching back at life.

I pulled my old Lower Merion High School cotton hoodie over my head and watched the candidates run. Maybe my coaching days were over. Maybe I was too lost to give advice. I sat, the turf damp with the coming chill of evening, and breathed in the rubbery smell of the track.

The man with the stopwatch walked toward me and motioned toward another officer. "We saw you running." When he spoke, the skin crinkled kindly around his eyes. "Lieutenant Smith says you should join the police. You seem pretty tough."

"Yeah, right," I laughed. "I just got smoked by a teenage girl." His was only a passing comment. Recruitment was, after all, his business. But it made me pause. Never in my life had I thought about becoming a police officer. It was not something anyone who graduated from a small liberal arts college even considered. It was too blue-collar. Too male. Too uneducated. "That would be some story," I said. "Exhausted forty-four-year-old mother of six-year-old-twins becomes a police officer."

"Stranger things have happened," the lieutenant said. Behind him, officers were unloading gym equipment. They rested a barbell on a cracked bench upholstered in shiny vintage red. A striped gymnastics mat—also circa 1973—stood folded in an upright Z. "Do you live in Montgomery County?" the lieutenant asked.

"No, Philadelphia."

"Too bad." He shook his head. "They do things different in big city law enforcement."

"You don't want me anyway. I've been told I have a bad attitude."

"The department might not want you," Lieutenant Smith continued, "but it needs you. Think about it."

I stood, raked my fingers through my wet ponytail, then waved good-bye.

Halfway across the parking lot, I paused and turned. The recruits had dispersed across the stations, each an independent part of a larger whole. I thought about the police. About Trayvon Martin. About how a week before a woman had been raped on the path I ran every day. Both these things made me angry. I could do something about them. I was pretty sure I'd be good police.

Being a mother was the loneliest of places. There was no team in motherhood. No finishing score. No high-fives. Even with the best partner in the world, as a mother, you weren't part of a group—at least not in any meaningful way where all members shared equal responsibility in the eyes of society. As Mom, the ball always stopped with me. Motherhood was an endless series of penalty kicks. Every goal was my fault. Every failure. Every forgotten homework assignment. Every broken bone. The first question people always asked when something happened to a child was, "Where was the mother?"

My car beeped open. *What a lark! What a plunge!* Mrs. Dalloway's words came to mind as I thought of becoming a police officer. So often now, I wanted out—to escape the monotony and terror of being a mother with twins who had been born prematurely. I groaned. It was only four o'clock. Leaning against the headrest, I thought about the nature of tests and remembered another athlete, one from two decades ago.

Emiko was a beautiful Japanese girl, all sinews and flow when she ran. She could win any event on the track, but when it came to the grind of a three-mile cross-country race, she caved beneath the weight of self-doubt. Then one day at Rose Tree Park in the town of Media, something changed. The sky was bruised and ominous when she sprinted across the finish line in first place, her ponytail streaking behind her like an exclamation point.

"Wow," I said, bowing my head against the spitting rain. "Just wow."

Emiko smiled. It was an odd smile, twisted at the edges as if she were no longer there.

"What did you do differently?" I asked her.

Emiko offered her hand to me. A long cut bit across her palm. She unfurled her other hand, which held a safety pin.

"Look," she announced, proud of something I didn't yet understand.

"What am I looking at?"

"I discovered this thing, Coach Megan," she said. "I ran with the safety pin. Every time I felt pain, or like I couldn't run any more, I stuck myself. The pain went away, and I could run faster."

"Ah, fuck." I turned her away from her teammates.

"What?" Emiko asked. When she was nervous, her accent returned.

"You can't do that."

"Why not?"

"It's not healthy."

"But I ran faster. I thought you'd be happy?"

"Running should be about loving your body." Before the words came out of my mouth, I knew they were a lie. I certainly didn't always run because I loved myself. I liked the pain. I liked the fact that running was a series of endlessly receding goals. It felt good to punish my body. There wasn't such a big difference between me running for five hours and Emiko's safety pin.

"But I love the winning," she said, hunching her shoulders against the sudden chill.

"It's not worth it, Emiko. You can't distract yourself from one pain by causing another." She hung her head, and I knew I'd lost her. "If I ever see you doing that again, Emiko, I'll throw you off the team."

If I'd been older when I coached Emiko, not in my twenties, maybe I would have done things differently. Talked to her parents. Said something about needing to live in the present, about needing to confront our stories and doubts as we lived them. Perhaps I might have said that some tests aren't worth passing. That day, when the rain rolled across Rose Tree Park, I said none of these things. Emiko sulked away from me, just another mutinous high school girl.

★ ★ ★

On the drive home from coaching Sarah at the Plymouth White-marsh track, stories and safety pins and failed coaching moments swirled in my head. I was furious at myself for listening to Nicky, for thinking that a child who had had three open-heart surgeries needed to learn how to embrace pain. The track had made me forget the part of myself that was a mother, the part that under-stood all too well that one's ability to withstand physical pain did not equate with mental strength. I didn't know if I would ever see Sarah and Nicky again. If I did, I would take her to the crushed gravel carriage trails of Forbidden Drive, where triangles of blue sky peaked through the canopy. Where she could run and walk when she wanted, and I would follow.

As I pulled into my driveway, I made a mental note to look up how one went about applying to the Philadelphia Police Department.

CHAPTER THREE

HAMMER TIME

DECEMBER 2014
MT. AIRY, PENNSYLVANIA

I DIDN'T KNOW IT THEN, driving home from the Plymouth White-marsh Track in the waning October sun, but my life changed that day. Lieutenant Smith gave me hope. For a brief moment, I imagined what it would be like to start again. From zero. To escape. To reinvent myself.

When evening settled, however, I was too tired to research the Philadelphia Police Department. For weeks I made the same excuses. Every night after the kids fell asleep, I collapsed in front of the television with my glass of white wine. My days began and ended wrung out, squeezed of energy.

Then, weeks later, Grace pushed me over the edge. That particular December morning started normally enough. Augie cooked pancakes, then left for a run. The twins sat at the dining room table doing homework. Our two mastiffs lay racked out on the cool kitchen floor, panting in the unexpected heat of an Indian summer. Windows and doors were flung open, the warm air bringing memories of sprinklers and popsicles. Gus was writing about *Fly Guy*. Grace had chosen *Llama Llama Mad at Mama*.

"Mommy," Gus said. "Can you help me?"

"Let me see it." I pulled his paper toward me. *I like Fli Guy*, he had scratched in large block letters. Every time I saw his writing, I was grateful. No matter how stuttered his pencil strokes were, or how full of misspellings his sentences, they always returned me to the postpartum brain scan that said he might not ever be able to hold a pencil or feed himself.

★ ★ ★

Two days after the twins had been born, Dr. Mark stopped Augie and me in the hallway outside the Neonatal Intensive Care Unit at the University of California, San Francisco. We were on our way to visit Gus and Grace, so small in their isolettes, their veins translucent, eyelids fused together. "We did an MRI on both your children," Dr. Mark announced. Still in my hospital gown and breathable postpartum mesh underwear, I propped myself against the wall. "Both kids have bleeding into the white matter of their brains," he said, apropos of nothing.

"What does that mean?" My hair was stringy, my body covered with the panic of bed rest and an emergency C-section.

"We don't know," he confessed. "But Baby A—"

"You mean Gus," Augie corrected. "Gus. That's his name. He's not a letter."

Our children were less than forty-eight hours old. We'd already spent enough time in the NICU to know the stakes were high. When Gus and Grace first arrived at twenty-nine weeks, weighing two and a half pounds each, they lay next to Baby Lila Hu, a giant eight-pound girl airlifted from the Central Valley. Lila's young parents started their stay jubilant and hopeful.

"She looks like a behemoth next to all the micro-preemies," her grandmother bragged. As evening became midnight and then day again, Lila's parents began to reflect their daughter's sunken look. Then Lila disappeared. The nurses stepped around her empty crib. *In the wake of Baby Hu's passing, her mother has asked to donate her breast milk*, someone had written in beautiful script on the chalk board in the break room.

"Right, right," Chief Resident Mark ignored Augie's naming of Gus. "Your baby boy is in worse shape than your daughter." He rustled the films in his hand. "He has significant bleeding into the white matter of his brain."

"What does that mean?" I snapped, frustrated by his singular ability to repeat this one damning phrase.

"We don't know. His motor skills will definitely be affected."

"Affected how?" My voice skittered down the halls. Lydia, the head nurse, stepped forward from her post, concerned.

"Will he be able to feed himself?" Augie asked.

"We don't know." A prematurely middle-aged man, overweight at thirty, Dr. Mark had the loose skin of a compulsive sweater. "He'll never be a concert pianist."

"Are you kidding me?" Augie set his jaw, and I stumbled, linoleum wall tiles cold against my back. In just two days, motherhood had toppled me. Upended, I cupped my abdomen, my physical separation from the twins raw, unbelievable. Once they were outside my body, I'd expected them to feel external, more distinct. Instead, the lines between them and me were more blurred. Motherhood was redrawing all my boundaries.

"We'll know more in a few weeks when we get another scan. Right now, I'm late for rounds." With a flick of his white coat, Dr. Mark vanished.

"What a colossal asshole," Augie said.

"Did he really just stop us in the hall to tell us our son is brain-damaged?" My words were dry, filled with the cottony taste of warm hospital ginger ale.

"Can I talk to you two?" Lydia padded toward us in white hospital sneakers. "Listen," she began, her voice low. "I heard what

Chief Resident Mark said to you. And I agree with you," she pointed to Augie with a smile. "He has the bedside manner of a sea slug."
We didn't laugh. "I've worked here for twenty years," she continued. "I've seen a lot of babies. Gus is going to be fine. There's nothing wrong with your son."

★ ★ ★

And so it was that when Gus's six-year-old hand grasped his pencil
and wrote *I like Fli Guy* on an unexpected summer's day in December, a weight lifted inside me.

"Homework is stupid." Grace threw her pencil across the room.

"Llama llama hates his mama," I joked, trying to salvage the
moment.

Grace poked a ragged hole through the llama's eye with her
pencil. "Llama llama no longer has to do his homework because
he's blind."

"Grace, let's put a Band-Aid on llama, finish up, then I'll jump
on the trampoline with you."

"Me, too?" Gus gamely traced his letters, ears on the alert for
all things gymnastic.

"No!" Now Grace was yelling. "I'm not doing it."

"Grace." Deep breath. Count to five. She was just testing me.
Again. "I'm fine with you not doing your homework, but you're
going to have to write a letter to your teacher."

"Mommy," Gus interrupted. "How do you make a lower-case 'g'?"

Grace peered over my shoulders. "Wow," she said. "Those letters are terrible, Gus." Gus's face crumbled.

"Go to your room," I ordered. Grace skipped upstairs, trium-
phant. I was raising a serial killer. In a few years, neighborhood cats
would start disappearing. Sweep. Thump. Thump. Grace was pulling
everything off her bedroom shelves. I walked upstairs. "Grace, I'm
going to lock your door if you don't stop."

"Fine." She plugged her ears. "Do that. Na-na na-na. I can't hear you. Na-na na-na nah."

"When you stop screaming," I hooked the chain outside her door, "you can come down again."

"Gus," I apologized to my sobbing son. "I'm sorry Grace is so mean."

"No, Mommy. She's right. My writing stinks." This slayed me to the core. I wanted to slap my daughter.

Of all the major decisions in my life, having children was the least examined. There certainly wasn't any test that said you should or shouldn't have children. The desire just was. It lived in the fibers and filaments of my soul. If you'd asked me in my twenties, after my second surgery for endometriosis, why I wanted kids, I might have said something saccharine about pets. About how there was a fierce love and kindness waiting inside me that only Otto, my twenty-five-pound Maine Coon cat, could touch as we pawed our way, one of us fully clawed, through the single years of my dissertation. Motherhood, in those days, was a theoretical proposition; it did not yet include the soul-crushing experience of having to protect my son from Twinzilla.

"Mommy," Grace called the moment I returned to the dining room table, all sweetness and light. "I'm ready to behave." I walked upstairs and unlocked her door, wishing for a different kind of motherhood—one that didn't require an external lock on my daughter's bedroom. Gus and I finished his sentences while Grace puttered around the house. She went into the basement; she walked upstairs. Then I heard the unmistakable sound of a hammer crashing through a wall. Stunned, Gus and I sat, suspended in our hope that there might be a rational explanation for those noises. Then I was hurdling the stairs three at a time.

Grace stopped, hammer poised mid-air. Then she whacked it with all her might against the door jamb. She was stripping the lock off the door. Too heavy for her six-year-old arms, every other swing missed, gouging huge holes in the wall. The mangled lock hung haphazardly off the door frame. Utterly depleted, I bowed before Grace, brilliant mastermind. She had pretended to be contrite, found a curved-claw hammer in the basement, brought it upstairs, and begun her own personal construction project—removing the hated lock. Faced with my daughter's evil genius, I was tempted to nod, give her a fist pump, and turn on my heels with a final "Respect. Peace out, dude." She'd won this round. I had nothing.

"Give me the hammer, Grace." She delivered it meekly, waiting for her punishment. Again, nothing. Punishment didn't work with Grace.

Spanking had no effect—beyond her asking, "Are you done now, Mommy?" I could ban electronics. She would dance and sing alone in her room. As usual, Grace left me drained, at a complete loss, outmaneuvered and bested by a first-grader. Again.

"Stay in your room until your father gets home," I whispered, so angry I couldn't yell anymore. "When he gets home, he can decide what to do with you."

Ten minutes later, Augie returned from his run. He squeezed his soaking shirt and draped it over our white picket fence while I recounted the morning. Even by Grace's standards, this was epic. The story left Augie bewildered, jolted. Any peace he might have found on the soft trails of the Wissahickon peeled away. "She's just testing you—," he began.

"From here on out, I'm auditing this class," I said.

"Grace," he shouted. "Come downstairs, please."

I passed Grace on the stairs and averted my face. She was walking to a spanking. We both knew this would accomplish nothing. There appeared to be some drywall work in both our futures. Outside my office, giant Norway Maples swayed. I heard Augie talking to Grace.

"Dangerous. Blah blah blah. You know better. Blah blah blah." Then the thudding run, the thwack, more screaming, a slammed bedroom door, sobbing. Within minutes, the howling became sniveling. Pretty soon Grace was singing. I now understood why some animals ate their young. A friend had recently told me about her sweet second-grader backing her into a corner with a kitchen knife and hissing, "Are you scared, Mommy? Are you scared?" Her story had made me think there was something wrong with her daughter, that I was lucky Grace wasn't violent. But the truth was that there was nothing wrong with either of our children. More mothers live these scenes than we would ever know. Because nobody writes them.

At the animal preserve the weekend before, Grace and I had patted the velvety nose of an abandoned fawn as the ranger explained that mother deer leave their fawns alone in fields for most of the day.

"How do I sign up for that parenting plan?" I'd interrupted. A mother standing next to me pulled her toddler son close and stepped away from me. I'd broken the first rule of Mom Club: you never talked about how much motherhood sucked. If you did, it was only with your best friend, in a moment of extreme desperation or drunkenness. Nobody wanted to hear that this sacred duty was actually a painful, personality-erasing, zombifying literal shit show.

"The babies get in trouble when people find them and think the moms have deserted them," the park ranger ignored me and continued. "But the moms don't leave. They just need food. So, if you see a fawn, leave it alone." Listening to the ranger, I thought human mothers should adopt this mother-deer lifestyle. My neighbors would be fine if Gus and Grace started wandering around like fawns, alone for most of the day because, well, sometimes Megan just needed to eat, finish an adult conversation, or go to the bathroom without an audience.

I hadn't signed up for the version of motherhood I was living. I was supposed to get Mrs. Brady. She had Alice, who was eternally present and, more to the point, always cheerful. In all the myths sold to me by our culture, I had backup. In real life, I got Grace, her hammer, and a husband who worked two hundred miles away during the week.

In my office, listening to the singsong voice of my young daughter in her room, my blank computer screen reproached me. It had been weeks since I'd tried to write. *If I only had a hammer, I'd hammer all over this land.* Grace now had her own theme song. My creativity was running on fumes and Pete Seeger. *Philadelphia Police Department,* I typed. I wish I could say that I thought about Trayvon Martin that day at the keyboard. About how righteous I was in my application because of the neighborhood rape. But no. I applied to become a police officer to get out of the fucking house and away from my children.

CHAPTER FOUR

MOMMY WORKING

DECEMBER 2014
MT. AIRY, PENNSYLVANIA

THE PHILADELPHIA POLICE DEPARTMENT website announced, *We are looking for the best and the brightest recruits to become a member of the fourth largest police department in the nation.* Ugh. Maybe this was the first test, I thought, my hand reaching for the mouse to correct the grammatical mistake. A stack of Christmas catalogs slid to the floor. Hanna Andersson landed face down. God, I hated that catalog. Being a mom was supposed to mimic turning its pages, each step a glossy new beginning. *Life Happens in Hanna.* A family in coordinated striped pajamas with matching happiness. Instead of this mythical world where a mother's primary worry was finding the softest, most durable organic fabric, I got brain bleeds and drywall projects.

What the hell. I kicked Hanna out of sight and clicked the application tab. Extra shiny slides of recruits being sworn into the department scrolled across the screen. Stern jaws, close-up details of badges, flags, lots of leather. Very *Triumph of the Will.* Something in me thrilled at the sight of these officers. "JoinPhillyPD: Be the Difference." According to the website, candidates had to be residents of Philadelphia and twenty-two at the time of appointment, with a maximum age of forty-nine. Before you began the series of admission tests, your application was accepted or denied based on a Preference Point system. One point for an Associate's Degree; three points for a Master's Degree, the highest educational standard listed. You could also receive three points for participating in the Police Explorers Cadet Program, thereby equating a program for teens with having earned an MBA or a JD. Three points for fluency in a language, which included Sign and Tagalog. Heavily weighted in favor of the military, veterans received ten points once they passed the written exam. Children of Philadelphia firefighters or police officers who were killed or died in the line of duty had ten points added once they completed the civil service entrance exam. The initial application took me two hours to complete.[1] I had to fill out every block for every job I'd had since I was eighteen. I uploaded an optional resume after some serious deleting. That article I'd once been so proud to publish about female incontinence in Renaissance drama? Not so relevant.

From behind her locked door, Grace sang softly to her stuffed animals. On the street below our house, neighbors walked toward the wooded trails of Fairmount Park. Children and dogs kicked leaves that had long ago lost their color. Augie walked out of the bathroom, toweling his hair dry. "What're you doing?" He shook his head, trying to free us both from the burden of Grace and her hammer.

"Applying to the Philadelphia Police Department." Startled by our voices, a squirrel paused midway up a nearby white pine to bark in warning, tail twitching.

---

[1] At the date of this writing, the PPD has removed the residency requirement. Applicants now have 18 months from their date of hire to move into the City of Philadelphia. In addition, applicants now need to be a minimum of 20 years of age on the date of appointment and have the equivalent of a high school diploma. The point system remains the same (https://www.joinphillypd.com).

"I don't think the police department wants someone like you," Augie said. "Grace doesn't get her personality from nowhere, you know."

"They need someone like me."

"They do," Augie conceded. "Whether the Philadelphia Police Department sees it that way, or not, is a whole different story. You're used to being in charge. In Philly, you won't get to be the drill sergeant in *Full Metal Jacket*. You'll be Vincent D'Onofrio."

I pressed SEND.

Over the next few weeks, as we moved toward Christmas, winter settled like a blanket over us and my application transformed into a party story. "Did Megan tell you what she did?" Augie asked at a neighborhood potluck. Inside the fieldstone house, we'd positioned ourselves next to the bar, looking out the bay window onto a snow-covered lawn bordered by winking paper-bag lights.

"Oh, no," voices chorused. "What did you do?"

"Hey," I raised both hands in defense.

"My wife has decided to join the Philadelphia Police Department," Augie announced.

"As in, you'll have a gun?" my friend Clarissa asked. In a group of investment bankers, lawyers, and doctors, this was the last thing anyone expected.

"If I get in."

"God help us."

"You know," someone added, "there are easier ways to get your husband in handcuffs than by joining the police department." Our friends snorted and snickered, enjoying an adult evening and the warm glow that came from anticipating the holidays with young children. There were many more jokes about Megan the Police Officer—mostly centered on my apparent dislike of authority—but the reaction from my peers was surprisingly positive. "Good for you," people clapped. "We need smart people."

We sipped Champagne and ate chestnuts wrapped in bacon. The talk turned to law enforcement in general.

"I mean, what's happening right now is appalling," Clarissa's husband said. "I can't imagine what it means to be Black in this country." Everyone nodded, affirming to one another that although we were privileged White liberals, Black Lives Mattered.

"Yes, but you still call 9-1-1," I interrupted, referring to a rash of recent break-ins.

"How's that relevant?" Clarissa demanded.

"Well. You don't hesitate to call if there's a problem. Would it ever occur to you *not* to call 9-1-1?"

"No," she admitted.

"So, you have faith in the system. As do we all." My hand circled, drawing the group close. Unsteady in my sequined dress and heels, I wasn't quite myself, my style more Private Gomer Pyle's sweatshirt covered in donut crumbs than Kate Spade. "That faith is one of the things pushing me to apply," I said, my cheeks flushed with Champagne.

"I just don't know if you're going to be able to deal with the police," another woman added. "As an Assistant D.A., I spend all day with them." She stopped to adjust the spaghetti straps on her black sheath dress. "I mean, some of them are great. The rest are knuckleheads. I can't even tell you."

"Can we now revisit the disturbing fact that you're going to have a gun?" Clarissa returned us to the beginning. "That is so hot."

The amount of attention I received at parties in the wake of my application to the PPD revealed another truth: Motherhood had made me dull and ordinary. I applied to the police department because I wanted to be extraordinary.

When Augie and I left San Francisco for Philadelphia in 2009, the year after the twins were born, I was cut adrift. Without a full-time teaching position or my all-women's racing team, I wandered through one adjunct teaching job after another. I'd already been lucky twice in academia. After doing the unheard of in 2004—giving up a Fulbright and a tenure-track job at the University of Rhode Island to move to San Francisco with my then-boyfriend Augie—I'd found a full-time lectureship at Santa Clara University. Academic success wasn't going to happen a third time—especially now that my children's health determined my schedule.

In Philadelphia, I bounced from part-time job to part-time job, going through the motions of teaching without ever putting down roots. I told myself this new schedule was great. I was free to spend more time with my children and to write. Except that I didn't write. I couldn't write. My days were clogged with diapers, doctor visits, temper tantrums. In Philadelphia, I was easily derailed. Even with the study door closed, my kids were like smoke—they always crept in, their presence choking me.

"Mommy!" Gus would shriek, escaping the babysitter I'd hired so I could have a few hours of uninterrupted work time. "Where's my Spiderman action figure?"

"Gus," I turned away from the computer where my cursor blinked at the beginning of an empty page, "I'm working."

"The one with no legs and no arms?"

"Gus!" I pointed to the door.

"I really really really need him!"

"If he had no legs and no arms, then I threw him out."

"You're the meanest mommy ever."

"Then leave me alone."

"Mean mommy mean mommy mean mommy." He rotated his arms to become a giant propeller, then bumped around the room, knocking into my books.

"Stop it." I stood between Gus and the shelves. My four thousand books were relics of a former life—alphabetized and organized by century, genre, and country.

"Okay, Gus," I walked him to the door. "I'm really really sorry I threw Spiderman in the trash. I'll never do it again. I love you dearly, but can you please let me work?" The missing Spiderman exposed one of the cardinal truths of motherhood: I would never, ever, be able to cull the endlessly reproducing herd of broken toys and molting stuffed animals. If I tried to remove a single one—perhaps by staging a fake lice epidemic that required everything to be bagged and removed—my children would notice and be unable to sleep, leaving me to dig through the garbage at 4 a.m.

In my pregnancy, I'd promised myself that there would be adult rooms in my house, that the baby sprawl of my friends' homes would never happen in mine. Baby registries were supposed to prepare women for motherhood. As new moms, we bought junk like wee-wee tents and bulb syringes, our purchases distracting us from the uncontrollable mess that is motherhood. But motherhood was the opposite of the baby shower; it was about trying to throw shit out, to detach yourself from all the broken Spidermans and incomplete Lego sets so that you had a room of your own. The two things you absolutely needed as a mother you couldn't buy on any registry— patience and space away from your children.

"Mommy," Gus smiled, a summer's worth of freckles still visible on his nose. "I like you better than the babysitter."

Whoomp. There it was. Whatever creative thought I'd had was wrecked, lying on the railbed of motherhood in a heap of smoking metal. No matter how many times I said it, Gus and Grace never understood the concept of MOMMY WORKING. On Monday mornings, Augie skipped out the door for work. But the minute I went to run, coach, or teach, a wild hurricane of howling assaulted me. As far as the twins were concerned, I already had a job—them.

The week before I applied to the academy, I'd brought the twins to collect my final papers at Philadelphia University. The day was full of emptiness. Students rolled bags across campus to Regional Rail, their heads burrowed inside scarves and down jackets, final papers replaced by thoughts of childhood bedrooms and home-cooked meals. In Philadelphia, students were always leaving me. As an adjunct, I never even had time to learn their names.

Loose staples and perforated paper edges littered the carpet of my classroom, signs of a semester that had ended too soon. Gus and Grace played on the floor as each student delivered a paper and said goodbye forever. "Who's the teacher for this class?" Gus asked.

"Me," I said.

"Ha ha, Mommy. No really. Who is it?"

"Mommy actually went to school for quite a long time to do this."

"No," Gus stopped to brush his bowl-cut bangs away from his eyes. "I don't think so." This was my son. Never in doubt, often wrong.

"I even have letters after my name," I said, my words not quite filling the abandoned room.

"So?"

"So, I'm really a doctor. My students call me Dr. Williams."

"Then cut me open when we get home. Here." He pointed to his stomach. "We can see what I ate for lunch."

"Well, I'm not that kind of doctor." I deflated. "Plus, I already know what you ate for lunch."

"Seeeee?" He drew the syllables out in the snide way of first-graders everywhere. "I knew you weren't the teacher."

By the time the twins were six years old, motherhood was all I knew. "Write what you know," I taught. Besides pithy Facebook posts and five-hundred-word blips on ScaryMommy.com, no one wanted to hear about real motherhood. It was sixty percent playground boredom, thirty percent overflowing happiness, and ten percent heart-stopping terror. According to the Hanna Andersson catalog and the Hallmark holiday that was Mother's Day, motherhood was sacred; it completed us as women. But these were flat-out lies, rhetoric meant to enforce the status quo. No matter what the Cult of the Blessed Virgin or the maternity clothes industry taught, being a mother in our society did not make you special.

Every Mother's Day, the Massage Envy website announced, "It's been a tough year for Mom. She deserves a little ME time." This advertisement made self-sacrifice the lynchpin of motherhood. Women were so used to erasing themselves as individuals, we needed permission from society to spend one day—one single day out of 365—thinking of ourselves.

Mother's Day rhetoric masked the reality that *every* year was tough as a mother. It was, essentially, a nonpaying job, but women were assumed to be either too in-love with their children or just too dumb to notice that it didn't come with a salary, benefits, or any time off. In our society, my biological imperative was to love being a mother; in a completely illogical equation, similar to Gus's wish for a life full of easy tests, this love made being a mom easy. On television and in magazines, motherhood was portrayed as the easiest of jobs—filled with French braids and remembering doctor's appointments—details so meaningless and natural that most fathers never needed to master them. Motherhood was a cultural construct, a Pampers commercial that never showed any mess or shit—least of all the massive blowout or the dreaded swim diaper.

When I told people I was a mostly stay-at-home mom, they'd ask, "But what's your real job?" or "What do you do with all your free time? Don't you get bored?" or "Don't you want to work?" or "When are you going to get a real career?" My answer to these questions was obvious: I told people I sat at home and ate bonbons on the couch all day because I was lazy.

Yes, I coached private running clients and taught college classes. I got out of the house, but Gus and Grace were all encompassing. Life was overrun by tiny suffocating details and an endless procession of snotty noses. Standing on the blacktop of a sweltering suburban playground, pushing Gus and Grace on the swings for the third straight hour, I'd once told another mother, "If I had a dollar for every brain cell I've lost here out of sheer boredom, I'd be rich."

"Really?" She edged away. Her three-year-old was wearing the Bright Basics Sundress in Organic Cotton with the Matching Underpants. My daughter was topless. "I just love it. Every single moment."

"Bullshit!" I wanted to scream, to rail against the rest of the mothers standing there smiling in their #blessed ways. "I'm calling bullshit on all of you."

I said nothing, and this was the last time I complained to a stranger. Maybe I was wrong. Maybe these women really did love all aspects of motherhood. My problem was that I didn't. Not all the time. And I wasn't allowed to say this. Nobody had told me that when I became a mother, I would always feel trapped. Conflicted. There would be moments—when I was rushing Gus to the hospital for double pneumonia or when Grace, overcome by a night terror, didn't recognize me—when I wanted to get the hell out of Dodge. In those times, parenthood was too big, the possibility of loss loomed too close. Nevertheless, I stayed, fear running smack into the immensity of my love for my children.

My plan when we moved to Philadelphia had been to become a writer, to publish that book I'd been imagining since sixth grade. But I didn't have an original story. I tried to write about in vitro fertilization and the twins being born at twenty-nine weeks, but sitting at my desk with their medical records—*Baby Boy A unresponsive and blue at birth*—left me paralyzed in a way that living the event never had.

"What are you writing, again?" friends at book club asked.

"About the NICU."

"Ah," they sipped their wine. "But didn't the kids turn out fine?"

"Yeah." People were always telling me my life would make a better story if something just a little bit more tragic had happened. "They're doing great."

"Hasn't someone else written about that?" my long-time friend Sue interrupted.

"Several people have," Jenny answered for me.

"Right. And wasn't there that woman who had the twins and one was born dead and she took pictures of it?" Sue added.

"Yeah, yeah, yeah." They all nodded, enthusiastic in their appetite for tragedy, particularly when it related to motherhood. I couldn't compete with this. Motherhood, as I was living it, was too physical, too constant in its daily assault. When I tried to write in Philadelphia, a long list of memoirs stopped me. Mary Karr's *Lit*. Dorothy Allison's *Bastard Out of Carolina*. *Darkness Visible* by William Styron. Timothy O'Brien's *The Things They Carried*. Alcoholism. Incest. Madness. War. These writers had real stories. My story wasn't enough.

Once, when I was still teaching at Santa Clara University, a student had asked if his ROTC leader could come talk to the class about Iraq. We were reading *Generation Kill*, Evan Wright's memoir about his experience as a reporter embedded with the Marines during the 2003 invasion.

"I guess," I'd waffled. We were studying a book about war, but we were also surrounded by palm trees and jasmine-covered adobe walls.

With red hair and an easy smile, Captain J.J. wasn't what I was expecting. When we introduced ourselves to the class, I mentioned my six-month-old twins.

"Jesus," he laughed. "So, you know what it's like to be in combat."

"Yeah, I don't think so," I said, even though I was so sleep deprived from feeding preemie twins every three hours that at a recent party, I hadn't been able to remember who Gus was named after. It wasn't a trick question: his father, his grandfather, and his great-grandfather.

"Look," Captain J.J. continued. "I've been to Fallujah and I have a four-month-old daughter. I know combat." His words warmed something forgotten inside me. Motherhood was war. The captain was saying I had a story.

But right now I needed a job.

CHAPTER FIVE

MY LIFE, IN DRUGS

NOVEMBER 2015
BACKGROUND INVESTIGATIVE UNIT
NICETOWN, PHILADELPHIA, PA

WHEN I ARRIVED HOME AFTER THE ACADEMY FITNESS TEST, the kids were playing Candy Land with Augie. "Can I see your gun?" Gus asked.

"I didn't get one yet."

"Does that mean you failed?"

"No. I passed, sweetie."

"Nice job, Mommy." Two breakfast plates sat, abandoned and forgotten, next to the game board. The kids' pancakes still held their animal shapes; a three-legged giraffe and a beheaded snake reminded me it wasn't even noon.

Augie moved the tokens away from the syrup. "Gus, stop cheating."

"You know, you don't actually get anything from winning at Candy Land, right?" I stacked the plates in the sink. "It's a game of chance. There's really no point to the whole game, so there's no point in cheating." The game required no reading or counting skills and zero strategy. Players didn't make choices. They only followed directions—an exercise not unlike my morning at the academy.

"You're wrong, and I'm winning." Augie flexed his muscles to show us what victory looked like. "Candy Land is about the glory."

Still chilled from the gym, I poured myself old coffee and sat. Plastic yellow, blue, red, and green game pieces flew everywhere.

"Did you read the rules?" I raised an eyebrow at Augie.

"No. We're making our own up as we go, right guys?" Augie drew Gus and Grace close. "We play full contact Candy Land."

"Super," I said, picking up a sponge. "That explains why the pieces are sticky."

Later that evening, I poured myself a glass of white wine, cozied between couch cushions, and opened the Personal Data Questionnaire.

"My job is to find out when you lie," Detective MacDonald had said, patting the stack of booklets fondly. "Trust me. I always find out. So do not lie. Tell the truth in this book." Several recruits nodded. One whispered that this was his second time through— MacDonald had already thrown him out once for lying.

Everything we'd ever done needed to go into the PDQ— starting with our first summer job in freshman year of high school. ESPN droned in the background while the dogs snored wetly on the couch next to me. The booklet was forty pages. Two pages were reserved for job experience. I was so old I was going to have to add pages. I'd worked since I was fourteen. Warburton's Bakery on Washington Street in Boston, yeast mixing with a winter's worth of stale air from the Park Street Subway Station. Going door-to-door for an environmental group the next summer, suburban towns blending together in one long butchered Native American word, NatickMattapanNeponset. As a cashier at DeLuca's Market on Charles Street, my white butcher's apron wrapped twice around my waist because I was training for my first year of college run-ning. Crystalline in memory, these places no longer existed. If I'd ever known my supervisors' last names, they'd long been forgotten, erased in a time before cell phones and the Internet.

30 for 30 switched to commercial, the story behind fantasy football thankfully eclipsed by an advertisement for Tide. "Let me see that." Augie grabbed the *PDQ*. My feet rested in his lap, both of us filled with the yellow warmth of a second glass of wine.

"Well, this is a shit show," he said, paging through the questions.

"I always said I wanted to write a book." The living room windows reflected us, soft silhouettes against the darkness of a November night. In the outside world, my garden was dead, put to bed—Blue Billow hydrangeas cut to the quick, once green Emerald hosta nothing more than frozen brown mounds. Inside this room, my life to-date was about to be compacted into a forty-page booklet. *I have measured out my life in coffee spoons.*

Augie stopped in the middle of the pamphlet. "What's Rohypnol?"

"Roofies."

"'Have you now or ever given anyone Rohypnol?'" he read. "Does anyone actually answer 'yes' to this question?"

"'Now or ever' makes even less sense."

"What's Ketamine?" Augie slid his hand through a perfectly cut hole in the middle of our alpaca blanket. "What is this?"

"Turn around." I pointed to the ledge behind him where a Breyer Clydesdale horse now sported a fitted alpaca coat. "Grace said he was cold. Ketamine is Special K—"

"You're not helping me here."

"It's a veterinarian drug, maybe a horse tranquilizer. You're awake and can't feel anything. It's a date-rape drug."

"Charming." Augie balanced the PDQ on his knees. My knowledge of these drugs was academic—learned at a Violence Against Women seminar at Santa Clara University. Against the deceptively soft background of the Diablo Mountains, we'd read statistic after statistic while doctors, social workers, and police officers taught us how to respond to students in crisis. When the seminar was finished, I'd driven from Silicon Valley to the winter that was a San Francisco summer. The dashboard thermometer ticked from ninety-eight to forty-five degrees, while chemical formulas and numbers remained, curdling in my stomach.

At the academy, Detective MacDonald had warned us that filling out the PDQ was a full-time job. The checklist of required documents was extensive: registration, title, insurance for all cars; vehicle records; security clearances; certified high school transcript. Rifling through the pages, I listed neighbors, references, all job supervisors, moving violations, everyone I knew who worked for the government. My answers filled the margins, but I left some pages blank. Gun use. Military service.

Halfway through our bottle of wine, the wind picked up, pushing fingers of cold through the window casements.

Augie read the next section. "'List all surgeries, doctors, prescription medications, and reasons for taking them.'" He paused then sliced his hands like an umpire. "And she's out."

"Come on. That was more than thirty years ago."

"T-R-I-L-A-F-O-N," I wrote, my handwriting neat, as if block letters could testify to my sanity, could outweigh Thorazine. My sophomore year of college, a breakup had blanched my world, draining it of color. I was barely able to drag myself to class. Heavy-duty antipsychotics had no impact. Nothing changed. One week, then two passed. Relentless days found me tracing the motions of living, trying to resurrect my memory of what it felt like to be human and alive. My doctor added the newly-released Prozac. Nothing. I packed my bags, prepared to drop out and commit myself. Two weeks to the day after starting Prozac, I woke up. Not a hundred percent better. Not even seventy-five, but the heavy gauze between me and life had lifted.

"Fuck." I rubbed my eyes and looked over Augie's shoulder into the blackness. A cold rain was now spitting against the side of the house. "Yeah, I'm done," I agreed. "The department will see an antipsychotic and that will be it."

"Maybe," Augie placed cold feet beneath the blanket. "Maybe not."

"If they know what Special K is, they're going to know Trilafon."

"They're going to be more concerned by what you're on now."

"On?" Defensiveness crept between us, sharpening the fuzzy edges of four glasses of wine. "I'm buzzed, not high. And move your fucking feet, they're freezing. No one cares about Prozac. It's like gum. Everyone uses it." I pushed his legs away. "Do you think I should lie?"

"Nooo." He elongated the syllables, weighing options, and turned to the next section. "Oh, goodie. 'Recreational drug use. Type, date, and amount.'"

M-U-S-H-R-O-O-M-S, I wrote. *May 1988. Maybe a bite-full (?).*

M-A-R-I-J-U-A-N-A: *ten times in my life. None in the last ten years. A shared bowl or joint.* The evening was closing in on midnight. Outside, ice glazed the bushes, their branches tapping together in the wind like bones. Upstairs, the children slept, unbothered. *30 for 30* had long ago ended. We were now in the doldrum hours of late-night television, the still-monotone waters that were indistinguishable from sleep.

"Bed," Augie announced.

"Yup," I agreed, closing the PDQ. "I'm done." Three hours. It had taken me three hours to finish—a single college-exam period—not the weeks Detective MacDonald had promised. Evidence of a life-lived ordinary.

I fell asleep quickly that night, only to be woken by the flat light that follows a storm and thoughts of the PDQ. "Your life in a booklet," MacDonald had promised. As a student, I'd filled countless blue books—hurriedly trying to transfer all my knowledge. My words overflowed. Only in the PDQ did I leave pages blank, questions unasked and unanswered. Up to this point, my life had been defined by the short essay, the place you could prepare for, where the important questions lived.

Somewhere in this application process, I wanted to be asked the critical questions: "What would you do if you were a member of a neighborhood watch in an affluent area and a young Black man walked past you at night?" I wanted some recognition of Trayvon Martin, of our shared historical moment. Instead, the *PDQ* asked about drug use. It segregated "prescription" drugs from "illegal" drugs, as if the OxyContin epidemic didn't exist. Where, among all these drug lists, was there a question about alcohol use? Where was there some recognition that alcohol abuse and dependence were part of police culture, brought on by stress and PTSD.[2] And when was someone going to pose the most basic question of all: "Why do you, a forty-five-year-old mother with a PhD in English, want to be a police officer?"

Eleven months after the fitness test, Angel called to schedule my background interview. Initially, my application had been marked as "incomplete" because I didn't fulfill the educational requirements. I hadn't submitted an official copy of my high school transcript, reasoning that college and graduate school were enough, that the department would understand that I couldn't have graduated from college without going to high school. Once I mailed my stamped high school transcript, I'd waited, mostly forgetting about the Philadelphia Police Department as the months passed.

---

[2]   In my research, I found a marked lack of high-quality empirical data about patterns of alcohol use in police officers from the past twenty years. A 2007 study found that about one in three of the respondents demonstrated one or more problem drinking behaviors (Butler Center for Research. "Alcohol Abuse Among Law Enforcement Officers." November 2015. "Hazelden Betty Ford Foundation"). In "Patterns and Predictors of Alcohol Use in Male and Female Urban Police Officers," 18.1 percent of male and 15.9 percent of female officers reported adverse effects from alcohol. 7.8 percent of the sample met criteria for lifetime alcohol abuse or dependence. This article calls for "prospective studies of police academy recruits as they enter police service, coupled with longitudinal designs permitting repeat assessments during police service in addition to surveying drinking behavior prior to joining the police force [*Am J Addict* 2011. 20 (10): 21-29]

At the academy, Angel had ferried us between classrooms, her voice gravelly, a mix of South Philly and pickup truck. She'd worn an unfitted pantsuit and four gold bracelets. On the phone, her bracelets jangled in the background as she repeated Detective Mac-Donald's first piece of advice, "Do not wear sweats."

My interview was scheduled for a cold Tuesday two weeks before Christmas. Exactly one interview outfit hung in my closet: a pin-striped blue French Connection suit that was my academic interview outfit. I'd last worn it to a funeral years ago. Wooly dust covered the shoulders and the pants hung shapeless and distended. I was pulling an undershirt over my head when Augie called.

"Did you smoke that doobie?" he asked.

"Next on the list," I laughed. "I'm currently fighting with an undershirt. My head is through the arm hole, and I think it might be on backwards." Everything Detective MacDonald and the other candidates had said indicated that this interview was going to be tough, perhaps the hardest of my life. I was prepared to sweat.

"That's a good look," Augie said. "Don't be late."

I hung up and tied my black shoes. With thick heels, they were spinster shoes, a revenge credit card purchase after a graduate-school breakup. I'd been twenty-six, with an annual salary of $12,000 a year and an older boyfriend who got me a Sears card for my birthday, saying I needed to "establish credit" and plan for my future the way he was, managing his parents' video store. The day I'd bought them, there'd been no reason for me to be in Suburban Square. No reason for me to pause outside Asta de Blue, except that I'd finally stopped crying and the door was open, the refrigerated boutique air mixing with a damp August, spilling waste and excess into the Square. The shoes sat in the window, alone and confident. They were ugly hulking things. They made me Emily Dickinson. They made me tall. When I wore them, my words dashed off the page. These shoes could kick down doors. Twenty years after I bought them, they still had the $180 price tag attached to the arch of the right sole, the only thing of value left from a two-year relationship.

Dressed, I made my way downstairs. It was a school day, and the house was preternaturally still. Our youngest dog Mia snoozed in the patchy winter light that leaked through the mullioned front hall windows. The minute my shoes hit the hardwood floor with a clomp, she sprang into attack mode—front legs spread and teeth bared—advancing in a crouch. One hundred and ten pounds of rescue mastiff.

"Jesus Christ." I reached out a hand. "It's just me, Mia." She padded over and sniffed my suit, ears wilting against her head when she realized I wasn't an intruder, just Mom in grown-up clothes. "You stupid fucking dog." I patted her torn ears.

On the two-mile drive to the recruiting office in Nicetown, the city changed from wooded hills to concrete demolition sites. At the top of Wissahickon Avenue, a beautiful skyline vista opened over an empty lot ringed by abandoned factories and stalled freight cars. Nine years of driving to Temple University had familiarized me with this neighborhood. Parking was a crap shoot, and garbage rustled down the streets like tumbleweeds. Street signs were defaced or stolen. I found a spot on Hunting Park Avenue, more worried that my car window would be smashed than of getting a ticket.

Half an hour early, I sat, the cold creeping into my car on a colorless morning. The 39th District was an active police station, as well as home to the Background Investigative Unit. Front doors swung open, releasing recruits in ill-fitting suits and men in dusty Carhartt pants. A red Subaru pulled behind me. Sam got out, shaking the wrinkles from her coat and rushed to my window.

"Thank God, someone from our old lady group is here. I'm a wreck."

"What?" I rolled my window down.

"The drugs." A light powder of foundation slid down her cheek and clung in the folds of her neck. "I have a history, you know—"

"What person in their forties doesn't?"

"I guess." She stood above my window, shivering and sweaty.

"It was the eighties. The past."

"The past?" Sam bent to fix her hair in my side mirror.

"Your drug use?"

"Oh, gosh yes." She lifted a hand to swat away history. "I have a goddamn kid."

"Where is he?"

"With my partner in Mt. Airy."

"How haven't we run into each other at the Co-op?"

"Right?" An unspoken knowledge settled between us. We could talk at the academy. We could talk on Hunting Park Avenue. But we would never have approached each other in Weaver's Way Cooperative Market. The center of our neighborhood, the magnet uniting us in shared liberalism, guilt, and privilege, it was a silent, strangled place. Neighbors didn't interact with neighbors in line at the Co-op. They judged what was in their hemp grocery bags.

Coming from San Francisco, Augie and I had worried we wouldn't be able to adjust to the conservatism of the Northeast. Our first weekend in Philadelphia, the city hit us with everything it had: soupy hundred-degree weather, thunderstorms that left clouds of gnats in their wake. After a day of unpacking boxes and trying to get jet-lagged one-year-olds to nap, we wanted soda.

We loaded the kids into the Double Bob, walked the three blocks to the Co-op, and asked the cashier, "Where's the Coke?" People picking organic kale and weighing lentils froze, paralyzed.

"I mean," I paused. "The kombucha?"

A collective sigh of relief swept through the crowded aisles, approving smiles rained down on us from the army of neighborhood women who lived in million-dollar houses, breastfed their six-year-olds, and endlessly debated the benefits of cloth diapers. Mt. Airy crunchy came in two flavors, real and faux. For every baby-wearing shopper with a Subaru that had long-crossed the 100,000-mile threshold, who made her own granola from the bulk oats and nuts in the Co-op barrels, there were two mothers whose Suburbans made weekly runs for tax-free wine in Delaware, who kept their kombucha in $10,000 refrigerators with custom panels, who would take the same hemp grocery bags to the Giant later that afternoon to pick up Cokes and individually packaged bags of chips.

"Mt. Airy is the best," Sam said, interrupting my memories.

"Ready to do this thing?" I pointed to the tired police station.

"I guess."

At the front desk, an officer buzzed us upstairs into a hallway filled with recruits. Wearing her signature pantsuit, Angel strode up and down, giving orders and leading individuals to be photographed and fingerprinted.

"Sign in there." With a clanging of her bracelets, she waved us toward a clipboard, then disappeared.

Hermetically sealed doors lined the hallway, each with an ominous sign. *Do not enter until called back.* Doors opened, and, one by one, recruits were pulled inside. Somehow the hallway managed to smell antiseptic and moldy at the same time. I toed a peeling linoleum tile back with my heel. They should have used more adhesive. More waiting. A door disgorged Detective MacDonald.

"Smith," he called. Smith was vacuumed up by Background Investigations.

"Relax your hands," a fingerprint tech yelled from a nearby alcove. Sam adjusted her shirt for the third time.

"Megan Williams?" An affable man wearing a brown shirt and tie appeared. He was my height, tan, with brown hair and brown eyes. Maybe South Pacific Islander or Hispanic. Definitely fifteen years younger than me.

I stood, whispered "good luck" to Sam, and walked through the door.

"Detective Brody," he said and turned away. Pictures of dogs and a woman with young kids hung above his computer.

"Those are beautiful dogs." I handed him my PDQ and supporting documents.

"Here you are." He spoke to a huge stack of files. "What we're going to do here is go through your PDQ, page by page." He folded over the first page and creased it down the middle with his thumb. "If I have any questions, you're here to answer them." He rifled through the beginning pages and stopped on drugs.

"Are these all prescription drugs?"

"Yes."

"They were prescribed by a doctor?" He ran his fingers down the long list.

"Yes." I pointed to my list of doctors.

"Well," he picked up his pen and cut a giant X across the page. "We'll just cross them all out then. Otherwise, it looks like you've done a lot of drugs. We're worried about the drugs people don't have prescriptions for." In an adjacent cubicle, Detective MacDonald sat hunched over an open PDQ, pen poised as he ticked his way through, line by line. A carpeted wall hid the recruit he was interviewing.

"Now," Detective Brody interrupted my wandering. "Now, we get to the fun part. You write here that you smoked pot in 1988." He paused for full effect, as if I'd just admitted I liked ripping the legs off kittens. "Do you remember how much?"

"How much what?"

"What quantity of marijuana did you ingest in 1988?"

"Uh, um—"

"A spliff? A dime bag? A bowl? A few puffs?"

"A few puffs?"

"Did you buy this marijuana in 1988?"

"No. Someone handed it to me. It was a reggae concert." On a still summer night on the Boston Commons, Jimmy Cliff sang about the rain clearing. Outside the pavilion, colonial lampposts blinked awake. The police swarmed everywhere, coming for me. I crushed the joint under my foot. A whole row of people leaned forward in slow-motion shock. To explain, I pointed to police no one else saw. After that, the row handed the joints around me. Twenty-seven years later, the police had returned.

"You took a joint from a stranger?" Detective Brody asked.

"Yes." I wanted to add a "fuck yeah" to my sentence, but this wasn't really an interview. There was no exchange of information here, no attempt to control a narrative, no acknowledgment that evaluation was happening on both sides of the table. Detective Brody was simply reading my blue book out loud. In 1988, I'd been eighteen, in love. It was so so fun and so so innocent. Of course, I smoked a joint at the Jimmy Cliff concert when someone handed it to me. Would you really want to work with anyone who didn't?

"You didn't write that." Detective Brody corrected something in the margins. "Initial here that I've changed it." I marked the page, and the opening of George Orwell's *1984* popped into my head. *It was a bright cold day in April, and the clocks were striking thirteen.* I'd wandered into an alternate universe where people cared what I'd done at a summer concert twenty-seven years before.

My mind wandered again. I was hungry. And bored. We needed groceries: Cheetos, fruit pouches, beef jerky, salt. Oh shit. All of a sudden, I was inside my spice cabinet. Smack in the middle was a bag from a decade old Mommy and Me party. *What the hell am I supposed to do with potpourri?* I'd thought, throwing the sachet bag above the sink. Weeks later, Augie found it and announced that the bag wasn't lavender. It was pot. For some reason, I had never thrown it away. Every Thanksgiving when searching for all-spice and other once-a-year ingredients, I picked up the bag and smiled. By now, it resembled desiccated seaweed, a reminder of just how square I was.

"We've never seen this before." Detective Brody pointed to the section on education and repeated himself. "We've never seen this before."

"What's 'this'?" I asked. Nothing like a good old pronoun reference problem to bring me back to the present.

"A transcript from Haverford College. You didn't really graduate with a hundred and fifty-seven credits."

"It says I did." I pointed to the embossed seal.

"They must do it differently over there." An insurmountable distance unraveled between the banks of the Schuylkill River, between a liberal arts college and the schools Detective Brody knew, between the City of Philadelphia and the Main Line. "Or they made a mistake."

"I took a lot of classes." Detective Brody wrote a giant looping question mark on the page, as if I were trying to pull a fast one, to get college credits I didn't deserve. "I really like school."

"We need an address for the Weavers," he said, switching gears.

"Didn't I give you one?" It wasn't like me to leave something out.

"It's a PO Box. I need a full address."

"They work for the FBI."

"I still need a full address." He pushed a piece of paper and a pencil across the desk.

"But they're secret agents. They don't want to be found."

Detective Brody folded his arms. "Work on it." I was noncompliant, lost in an endless loop of *Who's on First?* In all my rehearsals for this interview, I'd never expected we would come to an impasse over this. "We're finished." Detective Brody slapped the PDQ closed. Fifty-three minutes. Not the three hours Detective MacDonald had promised. "Hold on, hold on," Detective Brody gestured for me to stay seated. "I need to take a picture of your Facebook page, to make sure there are no, you know, pictures of you."

"My Facebook account is full of pictures."

"No, you know what I mean. You can't believe the number of people we catch partying with a bong, or naked." The detective pushed his computer toward me. "Log in to Facebook."

"Log in?" My phone remembered all my passwords. "Ugh, I don't know if I'm going to be able to remember."

While I scrolled through five passwords, Detective Brody turned chatty. "I just need to take a picture of your page, to make sure you're not wasted or something." Up came a picture of Grace and Gus outside a church.

"I no like churches," Gus had declared, refusing to enter for a friend's wedding. There were no sloppy drunks on my Facebook page. Detective Brody took a snapshot and stood.

"Oh, one last thing. How tall are you?"

"Five feet nine."

He ran his finger across a grid taped behind his computer and eyeballed me. "A hundred and ninety-six pounds. You should come in under that weight limit. Thanks for coming in."

I stood and picked up the PDQ.

"No," Detective Brody pulled the book away from me and put it back in the stack. "Your answers stay with us." The lock clicked shut between me and Background Investigations. I glided, unseen, down the stairs, past the desk sergeant, through the lobby. Outside the brick recruiting building, the air was heavy and foreboding. The forecast called for snow. Sam's car was still parked on the street. For two weeks, I'd carried around the PDQ, steeling myself for a three-hour interrogation. After less than an hour with Detective Brody, T.S. Eliot returned to my thoughts.

> For I have known them all already, known them all—
> Have known the evenings, mornings, afternoons,
> I have measured out my life with coffee spoons;

I'd expected challenges, difficult questions. Instead, I'd sat, bored, while Detective Brody paged through my life, as told in drugs. According to the police, I had measured out my life not with coffee spoons, but with twenty-seven-year-old doobies.

CHAPTER SIX

LISTENING TO PROZAC

DECEMBER 23, 2015
CITY OF PHILADELPHIA, EMPLOYEE MEDICAL SERVICES
FAIRMOUNT, PHILADELPHIA

EVEN THE MOST UNSYMPATHETIC OF SERGEANTS grimaced at the mention of the City of Philadelphia Employee Medical Services—a single-story brick building crouched on Nineteenth Street, defending North Philadelphia from the gentrification that was Fairmount. On this corner, I could get a no-soy no-whip latte from two upscale coffee bars. One block away, if someone in a hooded parka approached, I crossed the street.

"Be there before eight for your medical tests or you will be very, very sorry," Angel warned when she scheduled my appointment. Christmas was two days away. As with all things related to the Philadelphia Police Department, I had to be immediately available. It didn't matter that I had a house full of family or that my kids were on break. When the PPD said "jump," you didn't ask "how high?" You just gave your middling best effort. And you knew that wherever they sent you, there wouldn't be parking.

At 7:30 a.m., the wind lashed across Fairmount Avenue. Dog walkers with miniature schnauzers and toy poodles dressed in sweaters walked toward the Art Museum or Whole Foods. They never turned north along Eighteenth or Nineteenth Street. A city bus disgorged passengers outside the medical clinic, wrapping me in a momentary rush of warm air. Three men in puffy jackets waited with me in the cold outside the metal doors.

Half a block away, a patrol car idled. 7:59 a.m. A female officer exited, crushing her cigarette on the pavement. She thumped the passenger door. "Thanks for the ride."

My group didn't have badges. We'd blown into our hands and stomped our feet for thirty minutes, looking more like patients outside a methadone clinic than recruits.

At 8 a.m. on the dot, chains engaged and the metal garage doors ground open. Inside, the building was even more dismal than its profile. A receptionist shoved a clipboard at me. She was engrossed in the *Today Show* blaring from the waiting-room television. She trudged between offices, delivering paperwork and calling patients, orienting her whole person toward the screen.

"Look at this." She dropped my paperwork in my lap. "'Megan R. Williams.'" She shook her head.

"What?"

"Read the instructions." She was so close I could smell her drugstore perfume.

"It says *print your full name?*"

"Then you didn't fill this out correctly. You need to write out your full middle name on every single page. Don't you know your full name?" I stood, grabbed a pen from the basket next to the free condoms and signed my middle name on every page.

An hour later, my EKG took place in a windowless room.

"Pull your shirt up," the technician demanded. With cold hands, she stuck sensors across my chest and abdomen. The ceiling had brown swirls of water damage. My finger traced the outlines of a tornado or maybe a sticky bun while the machine measured my heart's electrical activity.

"All done." She detached the Tinker Toy leads, and the sound of a dot-matrix printer filled the room.

"Did I pass?"

"This part." She motioned me into the hearing test booth and handed me earphones. They were pillows of cracked leather surrounded by metal plates, circa 1980. "When you're ready, give me a thumbs-up." I raised a finger to start, half expecting to hear the pumping beat of Olivia Newton John's *Xanadu*, my first vinyl record. Instead, a vague series of muffled bleeps hummed, as if underwater. Then silence. And more silence.

"Is it over?" I opened the door. "That was really hard."

"It's supposed to be hard. The police have to hear things." With a swish of tan Dickie scrubs, she returned me to the lobby. Law enforcement officers, city employees, and recruits now filled the waiting room. Most of the candidates sat upright, folders ready. The police and firemen draped themselves over the chair backs, legs spread across the aisles, broadcasting their annoyance at being called for mandatory drug testing two days before Christmas. The air smelled of hand sanitizer. The television filled the silence, making real conversation impossible.

"Here are some toys that may soon be flying off the shelves, including Play All Day Elmo, who says a hundred and fifty different things." Matt Lauer promised us that "after the commercial break, Laurie Schacht of Toy Insider is in the TODAY studio with young helpers to showcase these toys."

The fireman next to me shifted, disappointed we'd have to wait through commercials to hear Play All Day Elmo.

For all the holiday talk spewing from the television, Christmas hadn't visited the Employee Medical Services. There was no recycled tinsel, no Secret Santa announcements, only bare carpet spots beneath every chair, marking hundreds of wasted hours. The staff was leaden. This, here, was life before Prozac.

A nurse called my name and motioned me down a cinderblock hallway. "Tie in front," he said, his voice a flat line. "Just so you know, this is a shared dressing room, so change behind there." He handed me a paper gown. The privacy screen in the corner reached my elbows. Half an hour and then an hour passed. My phone died. Three hours and counting.

Signs told me to put my gown in the hamper and not in the trash. There were six signs. Each with multiple exclamation points. Someone had taken the time to type and print each one of these, thinking, *Now here is a job worth doing.* I sank my head into my hands and waited. Employee Medical Services had won, beating back the hundreds of writers, books, and extraneous movie quotations that lived in my head. Now there was only silence.

Ninety more minutes. A knock on the door. "Come across the hall for the physical part of your physical," said a petite Black woman with *Janet* written in red cursive across the pocket of her scrubs. Janet took my blood pressure, weighed me, and tested my eyesight.

"Give me ten jumping jacks." I hopped and almost hit my head on the ceiling. *It's just a jump to the left. And then a step to the right.* Even with the door open, her windowless office oppressed, the walls close. Deep in the bowels of the building, everything was muffled, the hush interrupted only by running water and an occasional flush.

"Raise a leg," Janet said. I balanced barefoot on the cold linoleum floor, tempted to spread my arms like Ralph Macchio. *Wax on, wax off.* "Now run in place." I bobbed up and down for thirty seconds. Running nowhere. "Does anything hurt?" Janet asked, turning back to her checklist, her face devoid of concern.

"No."

"Anything else you want to tell me?"

I shook my head again. "No, I don't think so."

"You're going to need to come back for your drug tests."

"What?"

"You need a letter from your doctor because you're depressed."

"I am?" My arms crossed my chest, covering the rainbows and smiley faces on my bra.

She glanced toward the open door and whispered, "You're on Prozac."

"Yes," I agreed. "Since 1987."

Tight black curls framed her face as she folded my file shut. "Taking Prozac is a sign of depression."

"Since when?" I knew depression. Depression in college and then again in graduate school was waking up to falling. Putting one foot in front of the other, hoping that the next day would return me to the person I'd been. Depression was turning toward the chalkboard in Anderson Hall while I taught because my parents were getting divorced after thirty years of marriage, and I couldn't stop crying. For weeks I cried on the Temple University campus, feelings stale in my mouth. Day in and day out. In the evenings, waiting for the train home, thoughts of jumping filled the North Philadelphia platform. There were papers to grade. My twenty-three-pound cat. My new $180 shoes. These things meant something.

"Well." Janet sighed and opened my application again. "What should I put down as the reason you take Prozac?"

"Quality of life."

She wrote something in the margin. "You see a therapist?"

"Yes."

"Why?"

"What do you mean by 'why?'" I asked.

She paused long enough for the heat to cycle back on, then repeated the question. "Why do you talk to a therapist if you aren't depressed?"

"I'm a parent of seven-year-old twins." Lukewarm air blew through the vents, filling the room with old heat. "Sometimes I need a third opinion. You know, someone to talk to?"

She snapped my file shut. "Have your doctor fax this form. They won't drug test you until I've cleared you for the Prozac."

"I don't understand," I said, shivering in my underwear. "The department has known for over a year that I take Prozac. Why did I have to wait for five hours for you to tell me this? Why can't you blood test me now and I'll get the letter after?"

"They won't drug test you until I've cleared you for the Prozac," Janet repeated, stamping DENIED across my application.

Back in the dressing room, I threw my gown in the trash can. Not in the hamper, as I'd been told. Six times. With exclamation points. "Get that letter sent to Dr. Hasting as soon as possible," Janet called after me, her emotionless voice measuring the chances that my doctor would clear me for Prozac at less than zero.

That afternoon, Augie and I arrived home within minutes of each other. "I failed the physical," I announced before he had a chance to peel away the layers of December cold.

"Very funny." He unlaced his work boots, bluestone silt falling from the folds of his flannel pants. His cheeks were wind-burned and raw.

"Not joking," I said. Still cocooned inside my parka, my hood muffled my words.

"Why are you shivering?" he asked.

"I just spent five hours in a paper gown."

"You didn't really fail. There's no way—"

"Yeah, I did." I handed him the letter. "Look at the appeal I just had to pick up from my doctor."

"This floor is the best," he said, rubbing his feet across the heated tiles.

"Read the letter please."

"Okay, okay." He leaned over the counter. "*Megan Williams d.o.b. 11/20/1969 is currently under my medical care*," he read. "*She is treated for chronic depression and is doing well. I believe that she is medically and psychologically stable to join the police force.*" He rolled up his sleeves and the paper drifted out of his hands, landing in a bowl of Granny Smith apples. "What's wrong with that?"

"How would you like to be described as *chronically depressed* by a doctor you've seen twice for bronchitis?"

He turned to set a pot of water on the stove.

"Daddy's home," Grace ran into the kitchen, followed by Gus squealing, "Daddy, Daddy, Daddy!" Labrador retrievers, they wagged their puppy-dog tails in pure joy for Augie. Me, they greeted with tears, complaints, and an endless supply of pinch pots.

"Honey," Augie shook his leg where Grace was attached. "Why are you naked?" With a wiggle of her butt, Grace disappeared with a shout.

"Because I am, Daddy. Because I am." Bemused, we looked at each other and shrugged.

"What were we talking about, again?" Augie laughed.

Used to the scattered conversations that defined parenthood, I returned us to the site of our derailment. "How would you like to be described as *chronically depressed*?"

"Well, I don't get depressed, so I wouldn't know." He turned the stovetop knob. After a few warning clicks, it ignited with a woosh, consuming the dry air between us.

"Fuck you." The flame burned high and blue. "Turn that down. And I'm being serious."

"Is that a different diagnosis than being the parent of twins?" Augie asked.

"This isn't funny."

"Fine," he admitted. "No one wants to be described as *chronically depressed*. It has a huge stigma. Like you can't get your fat ass out of bed. And if you do, you can't get past the sock drawer, which you've been organizing by color for the past decade."

"Your description probably fits 99.9 percent of the people at Nineteenth and Fairmount—"

"It can't be worse than the DMV—"

"It makes the DMV look like an episode of *My Little Pony*—"

"The IRS?"

"No contest."

"Jesus." Augie dropped ice into a tumbler. "Drink?"

"Sure." The black pepper taste of tequila hit the back of my throat with a rush. "My doctor has seen me twice. Twice. Never for depression. We've never even talked about mental health. She refills a prescription I got thirty years ago."

Water boiled, fogging the windows from the inside and insulating me against the world of Nineteenth and Fairmount. "She doesn't want to be liable if you go out and shoot someone," Augie said.

"Chronically depressed people don't go out and shoot people. They crawl into a hole, molder for a while, then die. Like sick cats. Or they kill themselves—"

"Nice." Augie snapped spaghetti noodles and dropped them into the pot. The boiling water hissed and rattled the lid.

"To be honest," I said, removing the letter from the bowl of apples. "I wouldn't take me after this."

"Buddy," Augie wrapped his arms around my waist. "I'm sorry."

Gus galloped into the kitchen and stopped dead before us. "Ew, yuck."

"Gross," Grace agreed and pulled him up the stairs. The ceiling above us creaked beneath their game of hide-and-seek. Moments of silence, then shrieking brought with them a familiar claustrophobia. Parenthood at forty, after a lifetime of independence and ambition, was to be constantly circling back, a mouse in an ever-changing maze, running into roadblocks, trying to return to familiar places, only to find they no longer existed.

Deep in the second trimester of my pregnancy, motherhood first sunk its teeth into me—not with the teasing nip of a puppy, but with the steel jaws of a trap. Deemed "high risk" because of the twin pregnancy and my "advanced maternal age," at twenty-seven weeks I was no longer allowed to exercise or work. My world shrank, its borders close and recognizable. The couch swallowed weeks of my life. From the living room window, I could see the hospital lab that had gotten me pregnant. The ocean had rusted the round air vents on the side of the building, making brown tears. In the late days of my pregnancy, my body turned on me, became an alien, revolting thing. Each day brought some new ailment. The constant hangover signaled an impending brain aneurysm. Sharp abdominal pains were symptoms of appendicitis or miscarriage. One Saturday, on our way to a party in the East Bay, I wet my pants.

"You've probably just peed yourself," the triage nurse said. "Does it smell like urine?"

"It smells like wet cotton underpants."

She laughed. "Well, women with twins often become incontinent in the last trimester. You need to come in, just to be safe."

On the climb up Fourth Avenue to the University of California SF Medical Complex, the gloom of Parnassus Heights enveloped us. UCSF sprawled everywhere, a warren-like hodgepodge of interconnected buildings. The wind was blowing across the city from Marin—dry eucalyptus mixed with clammy salt water gusts. We didn't park in the emergency bay, entered the hospital gleeful, the sounds and smells of outdoors clinging to us. It was a spring Saturday in Northern California, and the hospital was deserted. A gift shop cashier painted her nails red while we waited for the elevator.

On the fifteenth floor, an obstetrics resident pointed to a gurney. "I'm Dr. Nelson. Lie down here." She was young, maybe thirty, and as she pulled on surgical gloves, her palms glowed white, fingers and forearms browned from biking in gloves. She shimmied my underwear down and swabbed the wetness that pooled beneath my lower back. "That's amniotic fluid," she said, a world of regret in her voice. "One of your membranes has ruptured. You aren't going anywhere for the next five weeks —"

"Five weeks? But only one of my membranes ruptured. You said 'membranes.' As in plural. With an −s. Doesn't that mean I have backup ones?"

"No." She oozed ultrasound gel across my abdomen. "Baby A's water has broken."

I swung my legs across the bed to stand, and she pushed me down. "We're admitting you. You're on bed rest until you deliver. A wheelchair will take you to your room. No walking for five weeks."

"Half an hour ago we thought we'd be going out for drinks tonight," Augie said.

Dr. Nelson shook her head. "I'm off for the next few days. Hopefully you'll still be here when I come back on shift." She collected my paperwork. "Think of it as a test. All you have to do is keep the babies inside."

During my exam, dusk had settled over the city. Twenty-stories below my hospital room, the Kezar Stadium lights flickered, following a few lonely Saturday night runners. For the next five weeks, my running team would practice below me, my bird's-eye view bringing not perspective but loss. A knock on the door interrupted my panic. Dr. Tran, the attending physician, had arrived to explain medications. Steroids to develop Gus's and Grace's lungs for an early delivery. Tocolytics to suppress labor. IV antibiotics to prevent infection.

"Why is this happening?"

"Sometimes membranes just rupture." Dr. Tran stretched two hands across her abdomen.

"But why?"

"Sometimes there's no reason." Her face was smooth and relaxed, revealing nothing. "We just have to hope you last the forty-eight hours it takes for the steroids to work."

"I just wanted to get everything set," I said. Stuck at home and in a rush to finish the nursery, I'd spent the previous day climbing up and down a fourteen-foot ladder patching holes.

"You didn't cause this." Dr. Tran adjusted the monitors on my stomach. "You sure don't look very pregnant." The sonic whoosh of the twins' heartbeats filled the room.

"Is that bad?"

"I can turn the sound off." She ignored my question.

"No, no. It makes me feel better." Dr. Tran closed the shades and darkness expanded into the room. On the pull-out couch next to me, Augie stretched out his legs and dozed, oblivious to the hospital sounds. Doors opened and closed, conversations between nurses and doctors disappeared around corners, medicine carts and IV poles rolled across linoleum floors, while I lay awake. At night, the hospital was a living organism. 1 a.m. The fetal heart rate monitor cast an aquatic glow across the white sheets of my bed. 2:01 a.m. The clock on the screen was relentless, a broken metronome, parsing out the minutes, each one slower than the last. At 3:07 a.m. every fluorescent light in the room blinked on. A nurse threaded a nasal cannula under my nose, another dug into my belly with the ultrasound wand.

"What's going on?" Augie squinted into the blinding lights.

"No heartbeat." The nurse shook her head at Dr. Tran.

"Let me try." Dr. Tran grabbed the ultrasound and cocked her head. "Nothing. Let's go" Someone lifted a knee to unlock the wheels of my bed. A hand pressed my shoulder. "Stay still."

"Who caught this?" Dr. Tran demanded as we rolled down the hall.
"Sarah."

I counted the joists between acoustic ceiling tiles.

"Nice catch," another headless voice chimed in.

Dr. Tran leaned over and spoke softly to me, her face bobbing as the gurney stuttered against the operating room doorway. "Baby B's heart rate is in rapid deceleration. We're prepping you for an emergency C-section. Do you understand?"

The operating room was cold and full of people unwrapping sterile instruments and untangling leads.

"Hi Megan." Another face bent in too close and smiled. "I'm Dr. Kamali. We're going to try to find Baby B's heart rate one last time. If we can't, you're going to go to sleep. When you wake up, the twins will have been born."

"Still thirty," a nurse declared. Doctors bustled around the room in preparation. "Wait. Wait." One finger stopped everything. "Climbing. Forty. Fifty. She's coming back."

"Keep watching," Dr. Tran said. "Yeah, she's back. Get a stool for the husband." Augie entered the OR wearing a sky-blue sterile jumpsuit, mask, and cap.

"Who invited the Smurf?" I wanted to know.

"Your daughter is a drama queen." Dr. Tran motioned to the half-opened surgical kit behind her. "She gave us quite a scare."

"What do babies born at twenty-nine weeks look like?" Augie asked.

"Better than babies born at twenty-eight weeks." Her back toward us, Dr. Tran covered the metal clamps and scissors with a drape. "Every day you keep them inside you equals a week in the NICU."

After thirty minutes of listening to Grace's heart, we returned to our room. Outside, dawn was streaking its fingers across the East Bay.

"I couldn't figure out what the hell was going on," Augie said. "I mean, I know it's a teaching hospital and everything, but I thought sending a gazillion people to take your vitals at 3 a.m. was a bit excessive."

I snorted, wanting to get beyond this. Four hours later, it happened again. Then again. And again. And again. Over the course of the next two days, I was rushed into the operating room seven times.

My father brought the Sunday *New York Times*, telling us it was ninety degrees outside, unseasonably warm for San Francisco in May. By that time, we'd lost Grace's heartbeat so many times, they'd moved me opposite OR #1. I no longer had a view of Kezar Stadium. Red-tailed hawks coasted on the updrafts above Twin Peaks, the scene cold and windswept. Only the stressed sounds of the HVAC system working overtime convinced me we were in the middle of a heatwave.

On the fifteenth floor of UCSF Benioff Children's Hospital, my daughter took me hostage. Medically, there was supposedly nothing wrong with her. Gus was the one in distress, his amniotic sac continually leaking and refilling. Grace's heart stopped when I walked to the bathroom. The nurses supplied a commode, and I lost the ability to close a door and cry. Then, Grace's heart rate plummeted when I sat on the commode. They wheeled it away and handed me a bed pan. Augie brought my computer, but the minute I sat up to read or type, Grace's heartbeat tanked and I was taken, again, to the OR.

"You might need to put those away for a while," Dr. Tran said, gesturing to my computer and books. After two days of having her lean in too close, I now knew that she was Chinese, that she was four months pregnant with her first. "Your daughter doesn't want a working mother," she said.

My body didn't understand bed rest. It continued to work, to hold on to the old Megan. On day three, my lungs filled with fluid from the inactivity. The doctors diagnosed pulmonary edema. Every two hours, I removed the oxygen mask for the nebulizer, exhaling hookah clouds of albuterol. "*You'll get used to it in time,*" the Caterpillar told Alice after she shrank. This was my new reality. Imprisoned in bed for five weeks, drowning in my own breath.

The fluorescent hallway lights outside my room never turned off. All day and all night, they buzzed and popped, while I stewed in the shrunken dark of my room. *God, please. Let the twins come early.* Motionless, I sat and I sat and I sat. Five weeks stretched away from me, each hour marked by contradiction. *Dear God, I'm sorry I said I wanted the twins born. Please let them stay inside for just one more day.*

On day five of my hospital stay, I went into active labor. "Can we just wait for my husband?" I pleaded with Dr. Tran as they wheeled me for the last time into the OR.

"Is he close?" No matter the crisis, Dr. Tran's face always remained ageless, unworried.

"He's on the Bay Bridge."

"Um, no. If he were in the cafeteria, I'd say we could try to wait." She swayed back and forth, debating. "Maybe."

Hands rolled me onto my side. A sponge drew a cold circle of Betadine on my back, then the needle sank into my spine with a crunch. A liquid sense of well-being flowed everywhere. I waved the anesthesiologist close.

"Will you marry me?" I asked, seeing his face for the first time.

Shaking her head slightly, Dr. Tran told him that no, I was not altered or special needs. This was me. Normally. People pulled and pushed around my abdomen.

"I can't get Baby A," one of the residents said. "Let me try." Hands dug deeper into my pelvis. "Nope. Me neither. Who has the smallest hands?" I craned my head, trying to see over the surgical curtain.

"I do." Dr. Tran dropped a shoulder into me. "Nope. He's crawled way down into the pelvis to get away from his sister." Minutes passed as Dr. Tran rooted around with both hands.

"Let me try this." She climbed onto the table, straddling me. "Got him." Fingers burrowed into me. "I think. Take him, take him." My son vanished through a chute into the NICU.

"Is he okay?" I asked.

"He's great," Dr. Tran said without making eye contact. "Great," it turned out, was a lie. Unresponsive at birth, Gus was born with an Apgar score of two out of ten. The nubs of his spine were black and blue from Grace pounding on him for twenty-eight weeks.

Compared to Gus, Grace was easily born. Her birth a portent, she called the shots, trapping me in the impossibility of motherhood—hamstrung between one child who wanted to be born and another who didn't. "If we didn't know Gus went from your belly straight to an isolette," the nurses told me that evening, "we'd call DHS on you." Six hours into motherhood, no longer stoned, I was being threatened with Child Protective Services.

With Gus and Grace gone from my body, my feeling of being confined expanded. My self, as I had known it, became secondary, ancillary to the outside lives of these two beings. As days turned into weeks, months, and then years with Gus and Grace, that bed rest panic never quite disappeared. The trap was always there, even if it was now balanced by moments of pure joy and a love so big I couldn't reach my arms around it. Maybe it would have been different if I hadn't lived a complete life before the twins. If I hadn't been quite so ambitious, quite so hungry. I'd been prepared to work hard as a mother. No one prepared me for all the times I would want to bolt.

"When Fiona was an infant," my sister Tamsen told me, "I'd leave her to walk around the block and catch my breath."

"You left her alone?"

"Had to. It was that or jump out the window. That oppressive feeling that you can't get out and it will never end. Right?"

"Yeah. I know it."

★ ★ ★

Two days before New Year's, Angel called me back to Employee Medical Services. Half-started Lego sets and small pieces of cheap wrapping paper lay scattered around the house, evidence that Christmas had come and gone, but nothing had changed at Nineteenth and Fairmount. Same blaring television. Same catatonic employees. Same plaid carpet. PPD, an acronym that spelled out both the Philadelphia Police Department and postpartum depression. An hour after my arrival, my doctor's signed letter in hand, Nurse Steve called me back to the changing room.

"Because of what happened the last time you were here," he lowered his voice mid-sentence. "I need to talk to my supervisor."

"Wait, what?" I unwrapped the paper gown and tried to find the arm holes. "What happened last time I was here?"

"With the Prozac?" he offered tentatively. "Let me give this letter to the Chief Medical Officer. She might want to talk to you." I cinched the gown around my waist.

Nurse Janet popped her head into the room. "Time for the body test."

"Again?" *Dammit, Janet. I love you.*

"Did you take the drug test before?" she asked.

"Oh. No."

"Right. Now open your gown and shake out your bra and underwear for me." A crooked C-section scar scrawled in bright red Sharpie across my abdomen, stuttering and starting. It wasn't tidy, and Janet looked away. "Now do the same thing with your back to me." She stamped something across my file and motioned down the hall. "You're cleared for hair." She pointed to another office where a heavy-set sergeant stuck labels on papers and ignored me.

"Did you take those photographs?" I entered the Chief Medical Officer's office and pointed to the wall.

"No. My daughter did." She continued to peel the backs off her labels.

"A long time ago I studied photography."

"Face the wall," she said. I scooted my chair to the side. She approached me with a comb and razor blade. "Move closer." She pushed my chair, jamming my knees into the cinder-block. "Sit still." The wall was now brush-stroke close. The sergeant stepped back and sighed in frustration. "You must sit still." As if I were a child, she cupped the back of my head and combed my hair. "Do. Not. Move." She sliced off a few hairs with economical violence.

"Why does the PPD take both hair and urine for the drug tests? Instead of just hair?" Faced with her silence, I couldn't stop talking. "I know hair testing is more expensive, but it goes further back in time, so doesn't it make the urine test redundant?"

"Because that's what the police department wants to do," she said, leafing through my paperwork. "You smoked pot fifteen times."

I nodded.

"You might want to rethink your answer to the possession question."

"I never bought or sold or owned pot. Every time I smoked, it was purely social. Someone handed it to me, then I passed it on."

"So you possessed it."

"If that's what possession means, then yes," I shrugged. "I guess I did."

"That's what possession means. You can go now." She stamped *PASSED* across my file. Just like that, pending the results of my drug tests, I was cleared. On my way out, a single photograph stopped me. Wedged between pictures of Logan Square and the Ben Franklin Bridge was a gate. *Arbeit Macht Frei.* Work will set you free. The sergeant had a picture of the gates of Auschwitz on her wall.

Thoughts about depression and pregnancy and motherhood swirled together. Auschwitz. Shit. Holocaust survivor Elie Wiesel had visited my high school when I was a sophomore. He stood in our small auditorium wearing a business suit that made me feel cheated. My fourteen-year-old self had wanted to see his tattoo—to discover if the writing on his body would imprint itself on me as strongly as his words had. He stood, not ten feet away, and read:

Never shall I forget that night, the first night in camp, which has turned my life into one long night, seven times cursed and seven times sealed. Never shall I forget that smoke.

The Ben Franklin Bridge on a shimmery summer evening. A metal gate. *Arbeit Macht Frei.* I no longer understood where I was or why I was here. This was a different kind of lost than motherhood. Feeling ill, I bolted from the office.

CHAPTER SEVEN

GUILTY UNTIL PROVEN INNOCENT

FEBRUARY 2016
THE INTELLIGENCE NETWORK, LAW OFFICES
17TH AND SPRUCE STREETS, PHILADELPHIA, PA

EIGHT WEEKS AFTER MY HEALTH EXAM, the PPD called to schedule my polygraph. In that time, the sting of Nineteenth and Fairmount had faded, eclipsed by the tiny escapes, the adventures that each step of the process offered. Maybe I'd been mistaken. Maybe I'd seen a different photograph that day in the sergeant's office. Since Christmas, the norovirus had cycled through our house, not once, but twice—a violent purging that emptied everything, leaving me with nothing more than the desire to get the hell out of Dodge, to bolt, to run, to trade my moral high ground for the chance to sit somewhere that didn't smell like vomit and bleach.

The polygraph appointment was a block away from Temple University's former Beaux Arts campus. My Chevy Tahoe ping-ponged down the narrow streets of Rittenhouse Square, hitting me with life's symmetry. Twenty years ago, I'd rushed into this same garage every Wednesday night, pushing papers and half-empty Gatorade bottles off the bench seat of my lime green pickup so the attendant could drive. In those days, after spending three hours studying nineteenth-century women writers, I'd been happy, in a solitary sort of way. The Center City campus of my past no longer existed. The basement den of classrooms and canted stairways had turned corporate.

Flanked by a store selling overpriced baby clothes, 1712 was an upscale row house. Inside, there were upholstered chairs, a creaky oak stairwell, a receptionist who treated me like a human being. This was a world I knew. My life had been full of interviews in this kind of office: boarding school, college, the Rhodes Scholarship.

A man in a hoodie and acid-washed jeans bounded in, followed by a hulking parole officer. The secretary motioned him over. Jumpy, he counted out $275, then man-spread across a sofa. A Hare Krishna mullet sprung from the back of his head.

"Do you think that's real?" he pointed to a paperweight from the World Trade Center Bombing debris that sat on the glass table. 1993. My second year in graduate school. We'd all been so innocent then, before 9/11 knocked our world sideways. "Do you think JFK splattered his brains everywhere?" The secretary flinched. The officer said nothing, accustomed to this kind of crazy.

Next to the paperweight, a stack of business cards told me I could learn more about this company, the Intelligence Network, at truthdoctor.com. A taproot of misgiving bloomed in my stomach. The lawyers at 1712 were not dusty academics. They might be ambulance chasers, scrappy personal injury lawyers, people advertising on buses and between afternoon soap operas.

"Megan Williams." A woman my age approached with a manila folder. "Amanda Fork. Sorry to be running late," she apologized. "Come on back." She was my height, wearing Boden's vintage wrap-around bamboo print dress that I'd circled a dozen times in the catalog. It was the one I'd buy if I had a real job.

Her office was a metal desk and two chairs. No personal effects. "Sit, sit," she motioned with a smile. I repositioned the chair so that we were face-to-face. "No, no." She pushed the chair back. "That needs to stay exactly where it is, because of the wiring." To make eye-contact, my torso now had to twist at an odd angle. Cords lay beneath the rubber floor mat. Years of criminals and recruits had buffed the varnish off the chair's elbows. The room was claustrophobic, a boarding school headmaster's office, heavy with the weight of impending punishment.

"I normally start this off by chatting, since the idea of a polygraph makes people so nervous," Amanda said. Her square jaw and blank expression made her look more Lego figure than person.

"I'm not nervous." It was the truth, even though the closed door and instruments transmitted a sense of wrongness, of mistakes about to be made, of lies told and forgotten on both sides of the table.

"You know my friends, Connie and Nicole." Amanda was referring to two of my references who worked for the city. Her tone possessive, they became her friends, as if we two were divorcing. She got Connie and Nicole. The dog stayed with me. "I run into Connie sometimes on the train," she continued. "Where do you live?"

We both understood she already knew the answer. "Mt. Airy," I said.

"Me too." Amanda and I had kids the same age, the same taste in local playgrounds. If we'd met at a summer barbecue, surrounded by sprinklers and the smell of warm potato salad, we might have become friends. "Great neighborhood." She flipped my file open. "You've got to be the most educated candidate I've ever interviewed."

"Thanks," I searched her face, remembering night classes, how much I'd loved school. "I think."

"No, no. It's great. You switching careers after so long. I did something similar when I moved from the D.A.'s office."

"I burnt out," I said. "I'd been teaching since I was twenty-two. That's a lot of papers."

"I get it." Her voice was soothing, charting the corners of congeniality. "Before we start, do you have any questions about the polygraph?"

"Why do you use it?"

"What do you mean?"

"Well, if it's not admissible in court, how can you use it to hire people?"

"Ah." Amanda balanced her chair on two legs, wrestling for control of the conversation. "I thought the same thing when I interviewed for this job. Then they polygraphed a group of us. It worked every time."

"They asked you the same questions about drugs and stuff you're going to ask me?"

"Well, no," she conceded. "They didn't give us the test you're going to get. They gave us pens. One of us hid her pen and lied about where it was. The test caught the person who was lying every time."

In that moment, I knew I would fail. Somewhere in the building the boiler kicked on, breeding hot air and adolescent resentment. I'd been in this place before, this room where my words meant nothing. This was every day at boarding school, where decisions were made by an irrational and invisible power. This was the lesson I'd learned my junior year at Westtown School, when I descended into the trunk room, looking for my blue Univega bike. I'd left home only two days before, but already homesickness stitched its way through my every action. I wanted to escape this school, with its curfews and study halls and roommates. I wanted to bike to Burger King. Not because I was hungry, but because its greasy smell could replace, if only for a moment, the manure that permeated everything in rural Pennsylvania.

Suitcases covered the windows of the trunk room, leaving only an occasional eyelash of light. Cobweb sheets draped over everything. Moldy comforters wrapped in plastic bags littered the floor. I kicked them aside, my sandal biting dry clay. My bike was gone. Stolen because I'd been dumb enough to leave it unlocked over the summer.

A hand grasped my arm from behind. I jumped. "Come with me," the headmaster said. My yearbook from that year contains several pictures of Master Rogers, none of them familiar to me now. Even then, he was more force than person, more feeling than image. His enjoyment. His hand pulling me. His leaden voice.

"Why?" I tried to pull away.

"We got a message that someone was smoking pot down here. I'm taking you to my office. If I go back and find any butts on the floor, you're gone. Expelled. On the next flight back to Boston. We'll give you an hour to pack your bags."

On the walk to his office, Master Rogers kept his hand cinched to my bicep. "Don't let her out of your sight," he told Teacher Heather, his secretary. Tears of confusion, anger, hurt clogged my throat. I would not cry in front of these people. I would not. I jammed my fists into my pockets, palming the quarters I'd saved to call my parents that evening.

"Can I go buy a Mello Yello?" I asked Teacher Heather. A former kindergarten teacher, Heather had abandoned whatever welcoming embrace she'd once possessed on the doorstep of her promotion. Moving the black slinky cord of her rotary phone so she wouldn't trip, she rose and followed me to the soda machine.

"Can I call my parents?" The quarters landed with loud plunks inside the machine.

"No." My soda came out sweating, fighting against an unusually hot September. The unopened can of Mello Yello sat in my lap while I waited in the office, both hands wrapped around it, an unwilling supplicant. Alone and afraid, I waited. Fellow classmates passed me on their way to buy frozen M&M's at the Belfry Cafe. Older students smirked as they left to smoke in the woods.

There would be no coming back from this. I didn't want to be expelled, even though I hated Westtown. My first year had been relentless in its intensity and monotony. Shy and spectacularly underdeveloped, I had two parallel lives—school days were shadowed by images of the life my family was living without me. Going to the cavernous red-carpeted movie theater on Charles Street where we'd seen *Star Wars* in 1977. Running on the Esplanade. Walking our puppy in the Boston fall. The scenes I created to torture myself were endless, but as the days passed, I learned how to live without my family. This was a peculiar kind of loss, tinged with extreme privilege. I grieved, but had nothing concrete to mourn.

My classmates were the opposite, celebrating life without parents. I had two friends. Evenings were spent learning how to study without my mother's editing eye. At the end of my first year, my friend Stephanie called to tell me I'd won highest grade point average for underclassmen. They'd announced the award when I was on the Mass Pike, my father driving the long road of summer home.

That day in the headmaster's office, I wanted to scream, to hit Master Rogers over the head with my award. To tell him I'd never smoked pot before, that my childhood bike had been stolen, that I was captain of the cross-country team—that even if I did smoke weed, I was fucking smart enough not to get caught. I said none of these things. None of them mattered. This was my new adult world: guilty until proven innocent. All I could do was wait for Master Rogers's report. So much depended on a dirt floor, packed hard by decades of students, beneath the empty dormitory rooms.

Master Rogers materialized in the doorway. "You can go," he waved me away. Teacher Heather returned to her paperwork and clunky phone. Tears started at the office door. For three days, I cried. For the rest of my life, I carried anger at myself for not fighting back, for feeling this guilt, this wrongness inside.

"The polygraph test was amazing." Amanda's perfect orthodontia pulled me back from the past. "Just incredible. I'd worked in court and never trusted polygraphs. After they did that test with the pen, I was sold."

"Let me get this straight," I said. "A hide-and-seek game with a pen sold you on the polygraph? Enough to determine whether a person gets a job?"

She turned to the blinking green cursor on her monitor. "I don't make that determination. I'm only one part of a very complicated process—"

"But if I fail the polygraph, I'm out from this whole application process." All the anger my fifteen-year-old self had kept inside was stacked behind my words.

"Well," she wavered. "You'd get to come back. Reading the results is multi-layered." Whoomp. There it was. The cog-in-the-wheel defense that had marked every step of the police application process. A true convert, Amanda continued to proselytize. "The department brought the polygraph back because corruption skyrocketed when they removed it. Corruption decreased when it returned."

"Yeah," I said. "But that was just an intuitive decision the commissioner made. At that time, he also increased the applicant age to twenty-one. There've been zero studies linking the polygraph to the number of police officers prosecuted for crimes. It's a flawed argument."

"We're ready to start." Amanda jiggled her watch. This was no longer an amiable meeting between Mt. Airy mothers. We'd been in her office with the door closed for thirty minutes. The boiler cycled off with a clang, leaving the room still.

"I'm going to attach you to the machine and explain what the test measures. Lean forward." Two girdle-like hoses crossed my chest and abdomen. "These are the pneumatic tubes. They measure your respiratory rate." She looped a blood pressure cuff over my upper arm. "This, of course, records your blood pressure and pulse. Give me your left hand." For a brief moment, our forefingers touched, God and man on the ceiling of the Sistine Chapel. Two metal plates covered my fingers. "These measure sweat." She arranged herself so she spoke to the computers. "There are pads under your feet that chart movement, so don't move. Are you comfortable?"

"No," I said. "The last time I was this hooked up to monitors, I wound up with twins."

She didn't laugh. "The test is ten questions that I'll ask you numerous times. But first, I'm going to ask you to lie to measure your response. How many fingers am I holding up?"

Her fingers swam in the periphery of my vision. "Three."

"Great. Now I'm going to ask you again, and I want you to lie."

"Four."

"No, you have to wait for me to ask."

"Oh, okay."

"How many fingers?" Amanda's hair didn't move when she spoke. It was an immovable brown helmet with ruler-straight bangs. I was being tested by a life-sized version of the tiny Lego pieces that lived between every couch cushion in my house.

"None." There were five.

"Okay. Good. Now we start the real test." She checked to make sure her wrap-around dress was tied. "Do I have your permission to tape this interview?"

"Yes."

"Perfect. Here we go." She grinned, a commercial pilot cleared for takeoff, about to gun the engines. "First question: Have you ever stolen anything from your place of work?"

"Of course."

"You need to answer yes or no. What did you steal?"

"A stapler. Maybe some Xerox paper?" Not all my memories of being a poor graduate student were good.

She shook her head, disappointed. "Let me rephrase. Have you ever stolen anything valuing more than $500 from your place of work?"

"No."

"Have you ever committed a crime?"

"Yes."

Her head shot up. "What was it?"

"I drove tipsy."

"A lot of people give that answer." Waving my confession aside, she gestured toward the ever-ubiquitous Personal Data Questionnaire from a year ago. "What about the pot here?"

"Well, you asked if I'd committed a single crime. Not to list all the crimes I've ever committed."

She sighed, exasperated. "Have you concealed anything in your application that might prohibit you from becoming a police officer?"

"No." On this I was definite.

"Have you knowingly associated with drug dealers or dealt drugs in the past five years?"

"No."

She paused before the next question. "Can anyone in your life say you've betrayed their trust?"

"Yes."

"Who?"

"My sister."

"What did you do?"

"Stuff any sibling does. Stole her clothes. Ratted her out. The usual."

"Have you ever betrayed anyone's trust as an adult?"

"Of course."

"Explain."

"Well, all that stuff with a sibling continues, you know, into your adult life. You still fight over your parents' attention."

"If you can't be more specific than that, then you need to answer *no*."

The rubber tube tightened around my chest, trapping me inside the ten-question world of the PPD, where everything was black and white, where life could be divided into yes or no. Here, there were no unanswerable questions. There was no mother in preterm labor asking, "Why is this happening?" There were no seven-year-old twins with the norovirus crying, "What is wrong with me?" In the polygraph world, when I didn't have an answer, Amanda cut and pasted her answers over mine, erasing my story.

"Have you ever betrayed anyone's trust as an adult?" she repeated.

"Yes. I cheated on my college boyfriend." What I didn't say was that we hadn't been dating at the time, but it still felt wrong, enough so that I told him. Eventually.

"That doesn't count," Amanda said. "As an adult."

"Um, okay." Of course there were people out there in the universe who believed I'd betrayed their trust. Big betrayals. Little ones. They made us human.

"What's your answer?" Amanda fiddled with her gold hoop earring. "Say it for the camera."

"Yes." What I heard instead from Amanda was "Say My Name." I blinked. Heisenberg. Channeling Walter White in my polygraph interview for the PPD wasn't ideal.

"Have you omitted anything from your answers?"

"Of course."

"Me ... gan." Her voice wrapped around my name, frustration pulling it into two syllables. "Answer yes or no."

"Yes," I said. "This test is only ten questions. My life can't be boiled down to that. By definition, I'm editing things out. Otherwise, we'd be here all day. I'm not trying to be difficult," I lied. "It's not personal. These aren't simple questions."

"They're supposed to be easy." She massaged the back of her neck. "Although the smartest people are the ones who fail most often, I have to grant you that."

"Well, that's a ringing endorsement for the test."

"The department does this so that they don't hire people who end up on magazine covers because of a shooting spree," Amanda reminded me.

"That seems to have worked out well for them on the national level."

"Take a moment to relax," she said, rolling her eyes at me. "Then we're going to go through the test again." She typed something into her computer. "Make that several times."

I groaned.

"Listen." Amanda raised both hands, abdicating all responsibility. "I like you. You'd be a great police officer. But you must pass this test."

"Okay." On the second time through, I fed Amanda the answers she wanted. "How was that?"

"I can't tell you how you're doing. I can only make suggestions."

"You're telling me I'm failing." I didn't believe in the lie detector test, but the idea that I might not pass it made me want to vomit. I didn't fail tests.

"You need to relax," she repeated. "You're breathing from your chest." She pointed to the pneumatic tube. "Breathe from your abdomen."

"My abdomen?"

"Yes." She sat up tall and motioned to her midsection. "Here."

"Ah," I said. "Like a fish. With gills. Except I'm a person."

She scowled before trying another tactic. "What are you thinking during the test?"

"Truthfully?"

"Of course."

"What to cook for dinner."

"Uh huh," she encouraged.

"And, if I'm being brutally honest, I'm bored."

"Well, you're very fidgety. The machine picks up on that. It's very sensitive."

"I'm not used to sitting still for this long."

Amanda and I ran through the test two more times before she powered down the machine. "I'm going to have to correlate these results by hand." She pulled a legal pad out of a drawer. "Right now, I would say that, no, you didn't pass. But I do need to score the test by hand. And I need you to explain your irregular results."

"Irregular?"

"Is there anything that would throw off your ability to take this? Did you have a good breakfast?"

"I guess." *Good* might be over-selling the cold English muffin Gus had pushed across the table, saying, "This is yucks. You have it, Mommy."

Amanda tapped her pencil on the desk, bringing me back from breakfast, from a different lifetime. "Did you get a good night's sleep?"

"I don't even know what that means anymore"

"It's six solid hours of uninterrupted sleep," Amanda said, helpfully.

"My son woke up four times last night."

"Is that normal?"

"Yes."

"Since when?" I shrugged her question away. Gus and his 3 a.m. Oreos had no place in this yes-or-no room.

"What questions am I failing?"

Amanda lay one hand on the monitor, a beige block of a thing not unlike my first Macintosh. "Whenever I asked you about drugs," she said, "the machine registered an irregularity—"

"An irregularity?" Her reliance on this word grated on me. It was clinical, dispassionate, something to hide behind. Every time she used it, I slid into a gynecologist's office, into discussions of periods and my inability to get pregnant.

"Your results are irregular," Amanda said, again.

"You mean it says I'm lying?"

"Based on your control questions, yes."

"My control questions about the made-up numbers?"

"The machine says you regularly consort with drug dealers," Amanda explained. "Do you want to add anything to your statement about that?" I wanted to ask about the machine, about its voice, about how it was now able to speak in complete sentences, to even use "consort," a word so formal and out of context it communicated nothing. Instead, I thought about pajamas. Ten pairs. I owned ten pairs of flannel pajamas. Most of them with small furry animals with pink tongues. The PPD must not have gotten the memo about my most unexciting of lives. In bed by nine, the only time I changed out of my pajamas was to go running. Pajamas on the drive to school. Pajamas at the grocery store. Ten pairs because of the endless vomit and snot. Hard to rule a drug kingdom in rabbit pajamas. Then again, a nice high school chemistry teacher turned an RV into a meth lab. Stranger things had happened. On television. Not in my most ordinary of lives.

Amanda cleared her throat and repeated the question. "Do you regularly consort with drug dealers?"

"I don't even know what that means," I said. "Drugs make me nervous. They're everywhere. My sixteen-year-old neighbor deals pot. Not to mention all the doctors I've met in my lifetime who probably over-prescribe." Amanda pulled a white cable-knit sweater across her shoulders. The overuse of prescription pain drugs was off-script, more than she was supposed to tackle in a ten-question test.

"Why didn't you mention your neighbor before?"

"It seemed stupid."

"Stupid how?"

"Well," I raised my hands. "I guess I did knowingly 'consort with a drug dealer.' Comments about the weather were exchanged when I took out my trash. Not bricks of cocaine. Listen," I said, fighting against past and present. Only once before in my life had my words meant so little. "I don't do drugs. I don't deal drugs. I don't know what else I can do to persuade you of this."

"Uh huh." She fished in her purse for lip balm then pushed a business card across the desk, avoiding my hand.

"Thanks." Doric columns decorated the front. "This is very judicial." A quotation on the back read, *For here we are not afraid to follow truth wherever it may lead.* The Intelligence Network didn't bother to attribute the quotation to a person. Or to finish it. Maybe Jefferson was too inflammatory in today's world, or maybe they were fine passing his words off as their own. In my line of work, they called this plagiarism.

I palmed the card. Thomas Jefferson wrote those words in 1820, a full hundred years before a UC Berkeley medical student and police officer invented the polygraph:

This institution will be based on the illimitable freedom of the human mind. For here we are not afraid to follow truth wherever it may lead, nor to tolerate any error so long as reason is left free to combat it.

Jefferson believed in language, in learning from mistakes. People, not machines, found the truth. By contrast, the polygraph spoke the language of the body; measurable physiological responses alone determined truth. Based on the Greek for "many writings," its name was a contradiction. The polygraph wasn't concerned with words or stories. It charted the body, ultimately exposing the myth that there could be a pattern of physiological reactions unique to lying.[3]

I put Amanda's card in my pocket and stood, yanking my torso free from the web of wires.

"Well," she said. "You have my card. Feel free to call me anytime with anything."

"When will I get the final results?"

"I'll start to review them tonight. The department should call you in a week or so."

"Then what? I'm not lying."

"Well, you never know." Amanda's plastic demeanor returned. "The machine is very sensitive. You could just be having a bad day."

"It's a pretty damn bad day if I'm telling the truth, a machine says I'm lying, and the people in authority believe the machine," I said. Amanda stood, her wrap dress draped unevenly in the static. "Open the pod bay doors, HAL," I wanted to scream into the void. But there was no point. Amanda's polygraph had a mythic identity—both machine and oracle, its inner workings were indiscernible to the human mind, its ruling final.

Nostalgia rushed over me. Graduate school was so much simpler than this. Studying, I could immerse myself in absurd worlds. The utopia of *Herland*. George Orwell's *1984:*

It was a bright cold day in April, and the clocks were striking thirteen ... Winston turned a switch and the voice sank

3   "The Truth About Lie Detectors." American Psychological Association, August 5, 2004. http://www.apa.org.

somewhat, though the words were still distinguishable. The instrument (the telescreen, it was called) could be dimmed, but there was no way of shutting it off completely.

These literary worlds were all encompassing, but they were fictional. There was no arguing with the PPD lie detector test. During the application process, I'd joked my way into a post-apocalyptic world—written myself into a dystopic corner both real and inexorable.

"You never know what the machine will pick up." Amanda gestured toward the box as she walked me to the door.

"You've heard of someone coming back for a second polygraph session?" I came to a full stop and faced her.

"Well, no," she admitted. "But stranger things have happened."

"Stranger than a forty-six-year-old housewife deciding she wants to be a police officer and then being told she can't because she regularly consorts with drug dealers?" I wanted to know.

"Thanks again for coming in." Amanda shut the door. The interview was over.

On the uneven brick sidewalk outside the office, the full import of my arrogance hit me. There would be no celebration that evening, no satisfaction at reaching the final stretch of the application process. Held hostage by a machine, I was out of the PPD. I felt sick, taking little comfort in today's final irony. Parked in the garage's cordoned-off area with the other "luxury" cars, the Tahoe was not my graduate school pickup, full of dings the attendants cataloged every Wednesday evening. I'd arrived. Sure, I'd been a bitch to Amanda. Maybe I felt bad about that. But the words I'd swallowed at Westtown had finally been spoken. I was a fully-functional adult. Even if I regularly consorted with drug dealers.

CHAPTER EIGHT

BREATHING ROOM

FEBRUARY 2016
PHILADELPHIA, PA

ON THE DRIVE HOME FROM THE POLYGRAPH, the Schuylkill River spread frozen beside Kelly Drive, a gray continuation of pavement. Philadelphia was encased in ice, its surface lunar.

"My interviewer basically called me a liar," I told Augie on the phone.

"Do you think this is part of their larger tactic?" he asked. A runner slipped on the towpath, cartwheeling to the ground in slow motion. She shook the sting away and turned home.

"Wait, what?" The runner had made me lose the thread of our conversation.

"Maybe the PPD wants you to learn what it feels like to be a victim?" Augie said. "To be wrongly accused? To feel empathy?"

"Right. Because empathy has characterized every step of this process." My voice skirted the edge between sniffles and hyper-ventilation.

"Take a breath." Papers rustled behind him. "If Gus can pass his car-seat test, you can pass the polygraph." The memory of the NICU threw everything into relief. Life was full of meaningless tests. Some you passed. Some you failed. The polygraph. The deep-end test when you were a varsity swimmer. The pregnancy test before IVF. The GRE subject test. The NICU discharge test.

★ ★ ★

As a teaching hospital, UCSF Medical Center outran the PPD in terms of its sheer volume of tests. MRIs for the brain bleeds. Bili-rubin for jaundice. Abdominal ultrasounds. Eye exams to rule out retinopathy of prematurity. Each tested us as parents, stealing a little bit of us at a time.

"What's that for?" I asked when a doctor came to dilate the twins' eyes. The chart on Grace's isolette read *Day 8 of life.* He'd walked past my chair to pick up Grace without introducing himself.

"A disorder of the developing blood vessels that can lead to blindness," he said. Never again would I look into the blue of my children's eyes in quite the same way.

Gus was tested the most. Once born, Grace proved herself a force to be reckoned with. She scooted around her isolette at night, grabbing the bottle from the nurse and guzzling the ounces. They were her ticket out.

"What did you eat when you were pregnant?" Nurse Lyd-ia asked one evening when Augie and I were rocking the twins, swaddled in warm blankets. It was week thirty-four. Six weeks until they were supposed to be born. Light was fading to purple over Parnassus Heights. Doctors glided from room to room, preparing for rounds.

"A lot of Jamba Juice and Budd's Ice Cream," I said. Grace's translucent hand inched up my chest, reaching. I tucked it beneath the blanket. "Dr. Robertson was worried I wasn't gaining enough weight, so I had to eat a bowl of ice cream every night."

"Hey, guess what?" Lydia said. Augie and I paused our rocking, waiting for the next test. "It's time for Grace to go home," she said.

"What?" I jolted upright. Asleep on my chest, Grace mewled her preemie cry.

"She doesn't need this anymore." Lydia removed the pulse oximeter from Grace's index finger. "She's been breathing well for quite some time." My daughter's naked finger terrified me. We'd been in the NICU for five weeks, its routine and rhythms defined the fabric of our days. The idea that I could hold my children in my own house, without the wires and constant stream of people, was unfathomable. No signing in at a front desk. No scrubbing beneath my finger nails with a disposable plastic brush. No public skin-to-skin contact. No need to ask the nurses' permission. In the NICU, we were chained to machines, always anticipating the flatline of respiratory distress.

"We don't usually discharge at thirty-four weeks," Lydia said. "But you know Grace. When she says it's time to go, *it's time to go*."

"But before discharge," Nurse Young added from across the room, "she needs to pass the car-seat test. She has to be able to sit for an hour without her vitals changing. You guys go to dinner." She waved us away. "We don't like the parents to be here." The nurses' idea of protecting us now, five weeks into our life in the NICU, was sweet but also laughable. Gus wasn't being strapped into an MRI tube, his face red with anger and betrayal. Grace wasn't having a feeding tube removed. For God's sake, I'd been present at their birth. Nominally.

The nurses imposed a clear and distinct hierarchy in the NICU. If you arrived at 8 a.m. and stayed all day, every day, as I did, they wouldn't make you leave for rounds, even though they were supposed to. The first and only time the doctors told me to leave, Nurse Young shooed them away. After that, students and doctors stepped around me. If a parent who never visited arrived five minutes before rounds, Nurse Young wouldn't allow them into the room, muttering under her breath that the NICU wasn't a babysitting service, that they didn't deserve to have a baby. The NICU, like life, was all about being present. The more you showed up, the more the nurses liked and supported you.

Following the initial shock of their delivery, the days passed inexorably. May turned into June, then July. Infection. Apnea. Bradycardia. Bronchopulmonary Dysplasia. In the face of all the medical jargon, all the tests, the twins grew, transferring from incubator to crib, the bubble-letter name signs Nurse Young had cut from construction paper fading in the summer light. The scuffed, beige walls of the NICU became home, the nurses family. I learned from Auntie Young, as she'd asked us to call her, that Nurse Olivia had fourteen-year-old twins born at UCSF, that Nurse Susan had a daughter killed in a freak four-wheeling accident. Auntie Young told me this in a murmur, as if she were speaking on a forbidden frequency. Death was a prohibited topic in the NICU. Life there was lived firmly, hour by hour. Any description of past tragedy might bring us closer to our own.

At thirty-four weeks, Gus and Grace were gargantuan, obscene in the amount they'd grown. We'd moved to the step-down unit, a big room filled with a drowsy yellowness. Six families shared the bay, two we never saw. The hospital hired baby cuddlers for these deserted newborns, ample retired women whose sole job it was to hold these babies, to let them know, even if it was just for an hour, that love could be tactile.

Stepping around the baby cuddlers, Lydia placed a car seat next to Grace's car seat. "Have two martinis at dinner," she advised. "We still need to talk about your son."

"What about him?" Augie asked.

Lydia adjusted the beanie on Gus's head. "Is he going to be upset he doesn't get to take the test?"

"You could have him take the test," Auntie Young suggested. "Even though he's going to fail."

"Have him take the test," I said. "We need to be fair."

"Yeah," Augie nodded "It sets a good precedent."

On our way to dinner, the wind blew up Ninth Avenue, briny and warm. For an hour we sat at the bar, returning to our single lives, forgetting about car seats and children. Friends were always telling us how stressful the NICU must be. No one talked about how freeing it was. Every night I left my babies. Dead tired, I didn't worry. Some NICU parents called to check on their children. Multiple times. We never did. Not once.

"It could have been really bad," my friend Sue said when I told her Grace was about to be discharged. "We were so scared for you. You didn't know all the horrible things that could happen at twenty-nine weeks. As doctors, Debbie, Jenny, and I knew. We made a conscious decision not to tell you."

That week, I'd dreamed that Sue was arguing with the chief resident. He'd insulted Gus and Grace by saying they weren't ready to come home because they had preemie heads. She was yelling, "There's nothing wrong with the DeLuca twins. They're perfect." I woke and knew they would be fine. They had to be.

On the night of the car seat test, a few fingers of light snuck between the buildings, grabbing summer, as we walked back to the hospital. The Sunset District should have been cloudy, socked in by a bone-chilling fog, but that summer had been uncharacteristically clear and hot. Outside the elevator bay on the fifteenth floor, we stopped. This anonymous hallway was the line of demarcation between two worlds—life inside the hospital and outside. For weeks we'd watched as the elevator doors slid open on tired faces, then closed around giddy couples, car seats in hand.

"I have some bad news," Lydia said, pulling us firmly into the world of the hospital. "Gus failed his car-seat test."

"It was pretty awful," Auntie Young added. "He turned purple the minute we buckled him. Then he screamed bloody murder. Didn't last thirty seconds. That kid's temper is going to serve him well in life, but his teenage years will be hell."

"How did Grace do?" I said, clawing through the cloud of two martinis.

"She was a champ." Auntie Young motioned to a pile of disconnected wires and sensors. "No issues. If she can sleep tonight without monitors, she goes home tomorrow."

In his bassinet, Gus was snuffling and stuttering, the way one does after a good cry or a great injustice.

"Sorry, bud." I lifted him from the cocoon of his blanket. Rocking him back to sleep, it struck me that failure was the first thing Lydia mentioned when we returned from dinner. Not Grace's success. But that was life. Sometimes, living in the present meant you got tangled up in life's little failures. Holding Gus, I wanted to scream, to emit my own piercing newborn shriek into the world, to protest the injustices of my pregnancy, the fact that my children were living in a hospital. Then I reminded myself that the car-seat test was just a stupid test.

In life, there were the real tests—parenthood and birth and breathing—and then there were the car-seat tests. You carried the results of the real tests with you everywhere. They lived inside your daily interactions; they were written on your body, in the C-section scar or a young athlete's trackside mutiny. Compared to the real tests, polygraphs and car seats were nothing more than distractions.

★ ★ ★

In the weeks following my failed polygraph, I changed wet sheets, wiped runny noses, worried that Gus was developing pneumonia. Random police sightings filled me with grief. This professional regret—this mourning over lost opportunities—was new. My past had left nothing on the table. The jobs I'd wanted were mine. University of Rhode Island. Santa Clara University. My races were fast. I was pushing fifty. My future would not hold a faster marathon or another scholarly book. Before the police, life had been tinged with professional disappointment only when a fellow-graduate student—or, even worse, the wife of an ex-boyfriend—published a best-selling novel. That name, on the cover, should have been mine.

Now, when I saw a police officer, failure slapped me: not tough enough, good enough, honest enough. I spent a lot of time at intersections thinking about breathing.

"Your breaths are too shallow," Amanda had advised during the polygraph. "Breathe deeply. Control your breathing." Five years in Northern California had taught me the language of breathing. During the polygraph, I'd slowed my breath, inhaling the claustrophobic smell of ink toner, dust, and pneumatic tubing. Paying attention to my breath made no difference. The machine read my body, spit out its verdict: drug dealer. The more you thought about breathing, the less natural it became.

Since the polygraph, everyone in my house had come down with a chest cold. "Jesus Christ," Augie said when Gus's coughing woke us at 3 a.m. "We live in a god-damned TB ward."

A chesty rattle accompanied my runs. Or maybe it was more like a whistle. I blamed the machine and the pneumatic tubing. And parenthood. Parenthood was an endless series of moments when the wind got knocked out of me. Gasping for breath, I pretended to be an adult. Childbirth classes spent so much time teaching us to breathe during labor. But birth was transitory. What we really needed as prospective mothers were breathing classes for the whole of our parenting futures.

For the first fourteen months of their lives, Gus and Grace had thrived in San Francisco. Their fat cheeks fooled us into believing the hospital was a thing of the past. Then we moved to Philadelphia, where Emergency Room triage soon knew us by name. We'd had five pneumonias and three hospitalizations in eighteen months. My kids were so sick in Pennsylvania, and I was so scared, I would have done anything—nursed them into adulthood—if it meant not having to watch them wheeze.

The signs of respiratory distress became part of our family's ver-
nacular: retractions, flared nostrils, stridor, blue fingertips. Each hard-
won breath came with a reprimand. Stupid. Naive. This was my fault.

Now, a few months after being called a liar, Gus woke us up at
3 a.m. with a scary-sounding cough. I telephoned the doctor. Augie
hovered in the doorway.

"Who is it this time, Mrs. Williams?" the on-call nurse asked.
Gus flopped across my chest. No longer the little bean he'd been in
the NICU, he labored for breath, head greasy with fever. I inhaled
deeply, determined that Gus could get more air by osmosis—that I
could become my son's iron lung.

"Gus," I said. These phone calls and interactions were so different
from UCSF, where a machine would bleep and Auntie Young came
to fix everything. Now, it was just me. Mom, nurse, monitor. Our
experience in the NICU had conditioned our every reaction to our
children, creating permanent neural pathways for us as parents. When
Grace got sick, anxiety surfaced, but not in the prickly electrified
way it did with Gus. From day one, Grace had imprinted us with
the sheer force of her will. She would fight anything. Even drywall.
When Gus got sick, all roads led to one place: the worst-case scenario.

"What's going on with Gus this morning?" Nurse Jen asked.
Disembodied fingers tapped across a keyboard, charting our conversation in real time.

"He's not really responsive," I said. "Coughing. Every time we
wake him, he falls back asleep. He never fully rouses."

"Wheezing?" The checklist began.

"Not that I can hear."

"Any stridor?"

"No, thank God." We knew croup and the sound of a child
barking.

"Nostrils flaring?"

"No."

"Retractions?"

"Can't tell. He's all ribs, all the time now."

The typing stopped. "Count his breaths for a minute."

As a runner, this was something I could do. Some runners survived the marathon by counting their breaths the whole race. They called it meditation. Afraid that the marathon would end but my counting wouldn't, I never ran this way.

"Ready? Set. Go," the nurse began. Sixty seconds measured many things. 300 meters around the track, an underwater lap of the pool, if we were emergency room-bound or needed to call an ambulance. "Stop," the nurse said. "What was it?"

"Sixty."

"Sixty? Are you sure?"

"I think so." In the face of Gus's lethargy, my confidence faded. "Maybe I should do it again?"

"No, that's fine." Then the commands began. "Head straight to the ER. And pack a bag."

Just like that, the wind was knocked out of me. Whoosh. I was on the ground, gulping for air. In the world beyond our house, the day was gray, its very ordinariness a rebuke. We'd been up for five hours, but our neighborhood was only just now waking. Cars backed out of driveways and children waited for the school bus, stomping their feet against the frozen ground. For weeks the East Coast had been trapped in a polar vortex—a snow globe of arctic air that held us motionless, shocked by the spiteful bite of being outside

"His respiratory rate should be 22 to 34 breaths per minute," Nurse Jen said. "He's in respiratory distress." I snapped my fingers at Augie, motioning in a familiar shorthand to put my phone charger and pajamas in the overnight bag. Augie would stay home with Grace, but first he wrapped Gus in a comforter and carried him to the car.

Key. Ignition. Shift. I drove and thought about the language of breathing. In English, we talked about breathing in idioms and metaphors. We "caught our breath," as if it were an elusive butterfly, waiting for us to cup our hands around it. We didn't "waste our breath" on things that didn't matter. Air was finite, measurable in its limited amounts. Skateboarders "caught air," as if it were quantifiable but rare. "We ran out of air," as if we were fuel-driven machines. "We lost our wind," "got the breath knocked out of us." All our words were about having or losing it. There was no middle ground.

At UCSF, the tocolytic drugs to suppress premature labor gave me pulmonary edema. My lungs filled with fluid. Propped up by pillows, mouth open, my wheezes came fast and quick, a cruel mimicry of labor. Lying there, unable to move, a childhood asthma ad surfaced in my thoughts. *Having an asthma attack is like being a fish out of water.* I was that orange goldfish, flailing, laboring for breath.

In scuba diving, the universal slash across the throat signaled you'd run out of air. Both Grace and Gus knew this gesture. They frequently gave it to me with their tongues stuck out. Done, Mommy. Throat slash. No more carrots. The last time I drained an oxygen tank, Augie and I were in Belize. The twins were three, at home with their grandparents. The diving boat hovered above us, deceptively close. My air started to thin. By the time I completed the safety stop at fifteen feet and kicked to the surface, exploding into the rough above-water world, I was sucking life through a straw. My ribs contracted, pulling from an empty tank.

"Why didn't you tell me you had no bars left?" Augie yelled, livid, as we bobbed along the surface. "Did you forget you're a mother now?"

I shrugged and inflated my buoyancy control device. "I dunno. I thought I could make it."

Speeding through lights on my way to the ER, I thought about running out of air. In life, air was thin, never fat. We always needed breathing room.

"Open his jacket so I can see him breathe," the triage nurse demanded from behind the glass. I shifted Gus to my hip and unzipped. He hung off my shoulder, immobile. Beneath his turtleneck, he was pulling for air. "Yeah," the nurse motioned to the door. "You guys are coming straight back. We need oxygen," she shouted. My breath caught, a momentary hitch. A gurney arrived. I lay down, pulling Gus on top of me so they could thread the nasal cannula over his lopsided ears. Someone attached a pulse oximeter to his finger. Gus's eyes fluttered. On any other day, he would have shrieked for joy to see his finger light up.

Another nurse slid a blood pressure cuff around Gus's arm. "Pulse ox 82," someone behind me announced. "Huh." The blood pressure cuff drooped. "I'm going to have to try a toddler cuff," the nurse said. "He's got some chicken arms." After X-rays and blood tests and nasal swabs, they wheeled us into our own curtained room.

The chief resident arrived. "Your son has RSV. Respiratory Syncytial Virus. Most preemies get it."

"But he got the Synagis shot," I said.

"When?"

"Every month until he turned one."

"He needed it longer." The chief resident bowed his head. "But insurance will never pay. And so we wind up with this." A technician appeared, holding up X-rays amidst the flurry of activity that preceded a hospital admission. Yes, Gus had double pneumonia. Deep breath, even though a plastic bag was settling around my head. Yes, they were admitting him. Breathe. Yes, he had a double ear infection. Yes, it usually took five full days for kids to kick RSV. The air was heavy with antiseptic and the maple syrup he'd spilled down the front of his pajamas.

The attending appeared. Dr. Smyra. I recognized her from the last time. She was chatty and wore a grosgrain headband. "All my wheezers were admitted this weekend." She patted Gus's head. "Must be something in the air."

I hated that she called my son a wheezer. Gus, my amazing son, boiled down to a label, reduced to his inability to breathe. Doctors listened not to his words, but to his crackles and rasps. This idea of air, that there was an invisible force, a vague "something" that changed Gus into a wheezer, terrified me.

"He looks pretty good," Dr. Smyra cocked her head. "For as sick as he is. He's fighting this virus quite well. Maybe because he's older. Some patients this week have been on all fours, head down, trying to get air into their bodies. Kids can stand a low oxygen level for several days. They do much better than adults."

Other doctors had told me this, each giving a different reason. Children tolerated thin air better because they were more resilient. Or because they didn't know how to say "I'm suffocating." Or, and this was the alternative that killed me, because they'd become so accustomed to it, they no longer noticed they couldn't breathe.

"Should I be scared?" I asked.

"I have two answers to that." She paused. "The first is as a doctor. No, your son has asthma. It's not like the seventies when asthma kept children out of school or benched during gym class. It's totally manageable these days."

"Super," I said. Being hospitalized on a Saturday morning did not make my list of "manageable" moments.

"My second answer to your question is as a mother," Dr. Smyra continued. "And, no, I wouldn't want my child to have asthma." This, it turned out, was the only answer that counted.

A nurse entered with our chart and ran through my medical history. Gus kicked at the sheet, exposing its pilled underbelly.

"So." The nurse straightened the sheet. "You're the one who gave Gus his lungs."

Her words filled me with guilt. I was a runner. I knew what gasping for breath was. At the end of a marathon, the wheezing feeling always crept in, a faint pulling of the stomach muscles around mile twenty-two as my body exhausted its glycogen stores and turned to muscle for energy. During a marathon, I chose to be without breath. Stop and my air returned. Gus had not chosen this. When I'd first become pregnant, I'd imagined all the wonderful things my children would inherit from me: my love of reading, my ability to run forever, my resilience. Never once had I considered the bad: my asthma, my OCD, my allergies, my depression.

"Our lungs are little sacs that need to be inflated." Dr. Smyra opened and closed her hands in explanation. Breakfast lay congealed, untouched, on a nearby tray. "Gus's problem is that he was born early. His sacs are still developing." I imagined little balloons inside Gus's chest unfurling like fiddle-head ferns. Outside the hospital, darkness leeched the light from the sky. Headlights along Easton Road turned piles of dirty snow an incandescent blue. People drove away from the hospital, toward a warm restaurant or movie. Pulling the covers over Gus, I shivered. There was no place as lonely as a hospital room on a Saturday morning in March.

My phone buzzed. I reached for it, knocking the straw out of Gus's sippy cup. Ginger ale. The taste of hospital. Backlit by fluorescent lights, my puffy face reflected off the screen. The hospital was never unlit, never quiet. This was the price of sickness. All night long it hummed and moaned. I smelled. Twelve hours without showering, coated with anxiety. An email popped up from Detective Brody.

Subject: Questiion in reference to Poly Result

Megan,

In your Pre-Test Admissions, you admitted that you ingested hallucinogenic "mushrooms" at a college party in 1998.

How many mushrooms did you ingest?

Det. Nick Brody

"Please Note: This Message contains confidential information of the City Of Philadelphia."

In a grim hospital room painted an exorcist green, I started laughing so hard I peed myself. The monitor flashed red.

"Everything okay?" Dr. Smyrna poked her head around the corner. I'd dislodged the pulse ox sensor from Gus's finger.

"Yes." I slipped the clip back on.

Why now with the hallucinogens? The PPD had known about these for over a year. During this time, they chose to obsess over my pot use. The quotation marks around *mushrooms* pushed me over the edge. And who didn't love a numbered list containing only one item? Or a stuttered typo in the subject line? Crying now, I tasted the salty exhaustion that comes with a child's hospitalization.

The PPD was fixated on my freshman year in college. I inhaled the happy memory of those "mushrooms." A spring day. The weekend between classes and final exams, when all of Haverford College came out to get stoned. The fleshy blooms of magnolias hung on the trees surrounding Founders Green, their cloying smell mixing with patchouli. My boyfriend, Tom, waved from the far side of the quad, pointing to a plastic bag and then to the library.

Compared to the tinny noise of transistor radios booming Bob Marley, the lobby of Magill was preternaturally quiet, punctuated by the dripping of the courtyard fountain. For some reason, which remained beyond my comprehension thirty years later as I lay in a hospital bed with my son, Tom and I had decided to take mushrooms for the first time in the library. The idea that it was dumb to eat hallucinogens before final exams similarly escaped me. We sat in the lobby's wool-flocked chairs, the mushrooms shriveled in our palms, their taste earthen. We ran back to the sunshine, giggling.

"You're so beautiful in the light," Tom told me, pulling me from the lawn onto his lap. Mushrooms made everything he said true. Then I noticed no one was working the snow-cone machine. We took over, and a line of people stretched away from us, mouths open like baby birds, arms clawing for paper cups. "So cold!" Tom exclaimed, up to his elbows in ice.

"I'll do the color," I said. Blue and red squirted from the bottles. The colors bled into each other, wondrous. "Oooh," I said. "Purple." The snow cones were my creation, the culmination of everything. This was the best day of my life. It ended at the Red Sea, an Ethiopian restaurant in West Philadelphia. There was a neon clock on the wall that kept moving, the concrete feel of wrapping cabbage with injera, staining my hands a dark yellow. Then the day faded to black and the shadow of a 9 a.m. French exam.

Gus coughed, interrupting the reel of memory. 1988. I was so young, taking the mushrooms so harmless. My thumb typed a response:

Subject: Re: Questiion in reference to Poly Result

Dear Detective Brody,

The date should have been 1988, not 1998 (sorry if that was my typo). I was a freshman in college, and that is the only other drug besides pot that I've done. I think I had two leaves about the size of a quarter each.

Please let me know if you have any further questions. I'm not sure where my application stands regarding the Poly right now.

Megan

Not two seconds later, the detective returned.

Subject: Questiion in reference to Poly Result

Megan,

How old were you when you did the mushrooms? Just to make it clear, you said 1998, correct?

I checked my outbox. Yes, I'd just sent an email answering both these questions. "I was eighteen, and it was 1988," I replied, siphoning the year, tasting its cultural touchstones. George Michael's *Faith*, Michael Jackson's *BAD*. Prozac had just been released in the United States, along with *Lethal Weapon* and *Fatal Attraction*, although the three were purportedly unconnected. Detective Brody wasn't old enough to remember any of these things.

The rubber hospital mattress squeaked. Haverfest had been *thirty years ago*, and the detective hadn't answered my question.

Subject: Questiion in reference to Poly Result

Dear Detective Brody,

I'm not sure if you saw my question at the end of one of my emails, but do you have any idea where my application stands? I was under the impression that I would need to take another polygraph, based on the results of the first.

Megan

Saturday became Sunday morning, marked by a dull ache between my shoulders. On Easton Road, the traffic lights blinked yellow. My phone beeped again.

Subject: Questiion in reference to Poly Result

Megan,

I have to put your file in for review (synopsis of all negative issues) and the supervisors make a decision to continue your process or end your process. If they decide to continue you through the process, you will then get a 2nd poly.

Det. Brody

Shifting Gus to my side, I typed my response.

Subject: Questiion in reference to Poly Result

Detective Brody,

Thank you for updating me on the process. In your email, you mention "all" of the negative issues in my application. I am aware that the polygraph is an issue, but I am hoping that you can apprise me of what the other negative issues are so that I can address them going forward.

Best, Megan

The detective's reply was immediate.

Subject: Questiion in reference to Poly Result

Just the drug use.

The flatness of his response annoyed me. As did his blanket "drug use." We were talking about the one time I did mushrooms when I was eighteen years old. Not a meth habit. Cradling my son who had double pneumonia, I couldn't imagine a candidate my age who had less of a drug record than I did. This I didn't need. Not now. Not ever.

I threw the phone down in disgust. An hour passed. Then another. My phone buzzed again.

Subject: Question in reference to Poly Result

Megan,

A few more questions.

1.) When you took the two leaves of mushrooms, was it at the same party?

2.) Did you take both leaves at the same exact time?

3.) How much time (minutes, hours) passed between when you took the mushrooms.

"Oh my God," I said.

Startled, Gus raised his head.

"You're in the hospital, Mommy's here." He settled back, long eyelashes drowsy. What could it possibly matter if I took the mushrooms at the same party or not? Was there truly a correct answer to this question, one that would qualify me to become a police officer? If only I'd known in 1988 how important those hallucinogens would be to my future. I would have acted differently. Would have counted the number of leaves. I certainly would have looked at my watch and logged my ingestion times. Being eighteen and in an *altered state* was no excuse. Propelled by failure and accusations and exhaustion, I couldn't stop myself from writing back. I wanted to win.

Subject: Question in reference to Poly Result

Hi Detective Brody. Yes, I took the two bites at the same party at the same time.

Megan

The next thing I knew, a nurse was tapping my shoulder. Rounds. Always at the ass-crack of dawn.

Gus opened his eyes with a giant smile, and I exhaled for the first time in two days.

"Now, there's a happy boy." Dr. Smyra warmed her stethoscope across her scrubs. "Gus, I'm going to listen to your lungs now." He nodded. This was familiar. "Wow," she said. "The course of this virus usually takes five days, but his lungs sound good. I might let you go home today if he can drink sixteen ounces."

"Home," Gus cheered, waving closed fists.

"Home," I agreed. For the next two hours, Gus refused every single drop of fluid. Water, ginger ale, apple juice. He sipped and spat, swatting my hand away. Not only had I not showered or eaten in twenty-four hours, I was now so sticky the hospital was going to have to treat me for a case of ants.

"I think we're staying another night," I told the doctor. Breakfast had come and gone. The Lutheran Church across the parking lot was ringing its bell, announcing Sunday services.

"He still feels pretty bad, I'm sure," Dr. Smyra said. "I wouldn't normally send a kid with RSV home, but you know what to do with the breathing."

"Yeah." I rubbed the crick in my neck. "Why don't I ever feel that confident?"

"That's just being a mom." She laughed. "Go take a walk."

We rode the glass elevator with Gus's cute little butt hanging out of his hospital gown. After one loop of the lobby, he glommed onto the gift shop. "Coke," he said.

"Yeah," I caved. "Sure." The boy did have double pneumonia, after all. I bought two bottles, one for him and one for me. Cold syrupy fizz filled my mouth, sugar replacing the taste of tired. Gus plopped down on the floor, both hands holding his bottle.

"Ha-choo!"

"Bless you," I wiped Coke off his face. He'd drunk so fast bubbles were running out of his nose.

"Hey, Mom." A girl walking across the lobby pointed. "That little boy is sick and he's drinking Coke."

"Mother of the year." I thumped my chest. "Yeah, that's right. That's me." The mother pulled her daughter's arm, afraid of the contagion that was my particular brand of parenting.

When we returned to pediatrics, Dr. Smyra was at the front desk scanning a chart. "How was it?"

"Awesome." Gus's voice echoed down the corridors of sick kids. "My mom is the best. She let me have my own Coke."

"How much?"

"All of it." Gus burped and held up the empty bottle.

"Wonderful." Dr. Smyra signed the chart in front of her. "Then let's start the paperwork to get you guys home."

"Wait, what?" Coke had caffeine in it. Caffeine was a diuretic. "Coke counts as a fluid?"

"Sure. Why not?" Her eyes twinkled. She was giving us a free pass.

When Gus and I left the hospital, the sun had replaced the thin light of morning, melting the night's blue snow, edging us toward spring. Gus was chattering up a storm, eyes bright. I unplugged my phone, determined not to waste another breath on Detective Brody and his hallucinogenic mushrooms.

CHAPTER NINE

WE GET TO DO THIS ONCE

APRIL 2016
BACKGROUND INVESTIGATIVE UNIT
NICETOWN, PHILADELPHIA, PA

IN THE DAYS FOLLOWING GUS'S HOSPITALIZATION, my memory of being a potential police recruit faded, not with a bang but a whimper. Weeks passed without hearing from Detective Brody. The first green shoots of spring appeared. On the last weekend in March, the claustrophobia of winter pushed my family outside. Gus and Grace collected sticks and pinecones, while Augie and I dug yard debris from beneath a glaze of ice and rock salt. The temperature was in the forties, but winter was still written in the soil, a layer of hoarfrost beneath the sodden leaves. I was on my knees, trying to scrape winter off our driveway, when *PPD* appeared on my phone. It was Angel.

"I'd like to schedule your psych evals," Angel announced, apropos of nothing.

"But I failed the polygraph." I threw my gloves in the wheelbarrow.

"I wouldn't be calling you if you'd failed." After twelve plus months of working with Angel, I kind of loved her. "Dress casual for the MMPI test," she said. "Business attire for the psychological interview." She disconnected without a goodbye.

My jeans were soaked, my knees raw from kneeling in dirty snow. I moved Augie's pitchfork into the garage, calling over my shoulder, "Let's make lunch."

"Yeah," he agreed, opening the back door. "I got chilled all of a sudden." While Augie reheated soup, I turned to Wikipedia. My phone told me that the MMPI, or Minnesota Multiphasic Personality Inventory Test, was used for people suspected of having mental health or other clinical issues. A series of true or false questions evaluated traits like "social introversion, hypochondrias, depression, hysteria, psychopathic deviations, masculinity or femininity, paranoia, phobias, obsessions, or anxiety."

"Cup or bowl?" Augie asked, ladling carrots, potatoes, and noodles for himself.

"Cup." I said. "The PPD says I passed the polygraph and have to take more tests."

"Oh, yeah?" Augie blew on his soup, making steam rise to his cheeks.

"Apparently, I have to prove I'm sane."

"Good luck with that." Augie slurped his soup. We were now in month seventeen of my application to the PPD. "Hey, are the kids still outside? Should we call them in?"

"Let's finish our lunch. I want to read you the sample questions."

His spoon scraped the bowl. A lackluster response.

"True or false," I read. "I am frequently/seldom bothered by diarrhea."

Augie lay down his spoon. "Megan."

"Um, that's what it says."

"Bullshit." He grabbed the phone from my hand and read the screen. "That must be a mistake." Now I had his attention. "Read the next one."

"Someone is trying to poison me."

"False." He waved toward the soup pot in explanation.

"I am afraid of spiders."

"True."

"You are not." I pushed thready pieces of celery to the side of my cup. "Why do you always put celery in soup when you know I can't stand it?"

"Because I like it. And I, too, am afraid of spiders."

"But when I yell, you always come and take them away." Even thinking about spiders, with their hairy faces and multiple eyes, made me shiver.

"They scare me less."

"Oh. That's nice."

"Moving on," he prompted.

"My father was a good man."

"True."

"See, I'd answer 'false' to that one," I said, curling my soggy paper napkin around a finger.

"What?" Augie frowned.

"No, stupid." I threw the napkin at his head. "Not because I don't like your dad. It's a verb tense issue. Your father *is* a good man."

"Don't overthink it," he cautioned.

"Right. We wouldn't want anyone with an attention to detail to become a police officer." I began to clear the table, stacking my cup inside his bowl. "Do you want my celery or should I give it to the dog?"

"Dog."

My celery landed on the floor, where Mia sniffed and then rejected it. The storm door slammed open with a bang.

"I'm hungry," Grace announced, climbing onto the kitchen stools. "What's for lunch?" She and Gus waited, puffed out in their parkas, two hatchlings incapable of feeding themselves.

"Grilled cheese," Augie said.

The MMPI took place on a Saturday in the Nicetown office. At 8 a.m., the neighborhood was deserted. Iron grates covered corner store doorways, collecting stray sheets of newspaper and waiting for urban renewal. The test was a twenty-minute non-event. Angel stood guard over the room while eight of us worked on computers. There weren't many questions about bowel movements. A few about arachnids.

"That's it?" I asked

"That's it," Angel said. I pressed send. "Business attire for the psychiatric. This is the end, the last test before the academy."

After the MMPI, friends, neighbors, and family reported police activity. Our family was on the couch drinking hot chocolate when Augie got the call.

"Do you know your wife has applied to the department?" the officer asked. It was flurrying outside, the last snowfall of the season.

Augie stuck a finger in his ear and walked into the hallway. "Sorry, what was that? I'm watching *Shrek* with my kids."

"Your wife has applied to the Philadelphia Police Department," the voice repeated. On the other side of our leaded glass windows, heavy white flakes settled on a dripping rhododendron, its buds already unfurling.

"Yes," Augie agreed.

"Are you supportive of her decision?" the voice asked.

"Yes," Augie said.

"Thank you. That's all I needed to know."

The police stopped my neighbor Hilary walking her dog Augustus. "I was kind of surprised to see the police at my doorstep," Deborah, who lived two houses down, confessed. My neighbor Steve popped his head over the fence we shared to tell me, "I didn't even know you were applying to the police department. They wanted to talk about your neighborliness." Locked inside the house, Shady and Mia barked.

Two neighbors who weren't on my list reported being interviewed, although there were probably more. Mt. Airy might have

the Co-op, but we still lived in an anonymous world, hidden behind screens and emojis. I could walk by the same house for ten
years and not know anything about its inhabitants except that they
owned a rabbit-eared television and a monochrome fuzz flickered
through their vinyl shades at all hours.

The police interest in my neighbors didn't make any sense to me.
It harkened back to a small-town Norman Rockwell world where
you knew your mailman's name and the complete history of the kid
bagging your groceries. It also introduced a level of context missing to
my application. No longer a number, now I was a woman who lived in
the stone farmhouse on Mt. Airy Avenue with a *Beware of Cane Corso*
sign. The neighborhood canvassing was extensive, time consuming, but
I wasn't sure what it accomplished that talking to me or looking at
Google Maps couldn't.[4] I was being profiled and I didn't like it.

The Saturday of my psychological evaluation brought a driving
rain. Augie and the twins were heading to their first 5K run. I'd
missed very few events in my children's lives. As Mom, I was always
there—for the pneumonia, for the first time Grace read a "big kid
book, with chapters and everything." Fidgeting with my keys in the
mudroom, I was on the edge of tears. My children had pulled me
through more life moments than they'd ever know. Boston 2014 in
the sleet. I would've stopped if Gus and Grace hadn't been at mile
22, standing next to the sign I still have that reads, *Go, Momy go!!!*

---

4   In terms of man-hours, vetting candidates for the PPD is hugely la-
bor-intensive. In 2022, *The Philadelphia Inquirer* reported that the PPD
spent "$11,000 on recruiting." It is unclear from the article if this is
per-applicant or the total cost ("Philadelphia's Police Should Look Like
Philadelphia," *Philadelphia Inquirer* 12 April 2022). In 2022, the PPD invited 3,800 applicants to orientation. 900 showed up. More than 500 failed
the reading or agility test. More were eliminated after drug tests, background tests, and psych ed evaluations. The Department offered jobs to
sixty-five people. Forty-eight started at the Academy. Forty-one graduated
("The Future of Work" by Anna Orso and Ryan W. Briggs, *The Philadelphia Inquirer,* 29 August 2022).

"Are you worried about this test?" Augie asked, zipping jackets. Puddles and clouds of steam dotted the frozen backyard. Inside the warm cocoon of our house, the detritus of a family was everywhere, in every cubby and on every counter. Mismatched mittens, paddle tennis rackets, a single sock with the pom-pom chewed off, a deflated pool donut.

"Not really," I said. "How about you?" I poked Grace.

"Ow, Daddy, stop," Grace shook her head, pulling her pig-tails inside the red hood of her raincoat. "You're pulling my hair." Her jacket was a hand-me-down, two sizes too big, carrying the Sharpie name of a boy we'd never met. "Mommy—?" she asked, only her white nose visible beneath the pointed visor.

"Yes, my little garden gnome?"

"I'm not little." She leaned against the closet door, closing it with a bang. "Gus and I want to talk to you about this." She motioned with her chin toward the weather. "We don't want you to run Boston this year."

"What?" Branches scraped across the window pane in the wind.

"It always rains," Grace said.

"Plus, you never win," Gus added.

"Um, yeah," I said. "Okay." Pulling my jacket around me, I slipped out the back door without hugging them good luck.

At the recruiting office, the rain, heavy and damp, couldn't mask the cloying smell of industrial cleaner. "Megan Williams?" A woman sat behind a desk and motioned me forward. She wore a pink sweatsuit with rhinestone seams, and her nails were painted a matching coral. Heat blasted from a clanging radiator. *Saigon, shit.* Willard's voiceover from the beginning of *Apocalypse Now* surfaced in my brain. *I'm still only in Saigon. Every time I think I'm going to wake up back in the jungle.* At the far end of the conference room, a window was open. A shade, curled a fly-paper yellow, banged in the wind.

"Nice weather," I said.

"Yes," the woman said. "Dr. Rosenberger." It was a statement of fact, not an introduction.

"I feel so bad," I said, making conversation as the rain beat down. "My kids are running a 5K race in this."

"Alone?" She moved her tape recorder flush against the side of the desk.

"With my husband." The window casement rattled.

"I'm going to close that." Dr. Rosenberger pointed to the window. "It's distracting. Aren't your kids a little young to be running three miles?" Standing, she couldn't have been more than four feet six. Her arms waved across the window opening, too short to catch the handle. I got up to help. Inside my head, the soundtrack continued. *This is the end, beautiful friend. This is the end, my only friend, the end.* I pulled on the window sash, wondering what it meant that *Apocalypse Now* was stuck in my brain.

"The race is for charity. They can walk it." The window was swollen open. "This isn't budging," I said. Splinters of wood and paint cut my fingers.

"Leave it." Dr. Rosenberger waved me back to my brown folding chair. "Are you ready to start?" A clock on the wall behind her ticked over. 9 a.m. The airhorn would just now be sounding to start the race, Gus and Grace slipping on wet grass, following a path marked by flour arrows.

"Why do you want to become a police officer?" Dr. Rosenberger asked.

"There's been a lot of crime in my neighborhood. A rape on a nearby trail. A lot of break-ins. I want to give back to my community." Instead of my voice, I heard Private Joker. *I wanted to see exotic Vietnam ... the crown jewel of Southeast Asia. I wanted to meet interesting and stimulating people of an ancient culture and ... kill them.* Dr. Rosenberger frowned at the word "rape," then moved on, leaving me with the questions she should have asked, the ones I twisted myself around, tossing and turning at night. One image, in particular, thrilled me: There I was, shouting, then kicking down someone's front door. The scene rolled, a marble inside my head, leading me back to the hard questions, the questions to which I didn't have answers.

How angry was I, really, at my life? I was forty-seven, and yet there were days as a mother that broke me. On the couch with Gus and Grace, home sick with the stomach flu for three straight days. *Alvin and the Chipmunks* playing, the shrill chatter of the original, *The Squeakquel, Chipwrecked,* and *The Road Chip* merging together, an endless loop of talking rodents. Surely this was the definition of insanity. Outside, snow fell beautifully, long sheets of it cutting across our hemlocks. As a kid in Watertown, Massachusetts, snow days were sneaking with Rachel Salzman onto the Oakley golf course with our toboggans. Graduate school snow days were spent wrapped in a book and a quilt in my attic apartment, insulated from the world. Those winter days were so different from the ones I had as a parent, trapped between the mind-numbing boredom of "Aaaalviiiin!" and my panic. Sometimes being a parent meant wanting to hit something. Instead, I pulled my boots on, dry heaved, and shoveled the driveway so we could leave for yet another doctor's visit.

Party jokes about handcuffing my husband to the bed aside, how much did the idea of being in power, of wearing a uniform and carrying a gun, excite me? Did I really feel this powerless in my everyday life? Yes. Viscerally, this would be my answer were Dr. Rosenberger to ask. Or maybe just sometimes. Not every day. But, yes. There were more days than I could count that knocked me sideways. *Alvin and the Chipmunks* was the soundtrack to my life as a mother. Its high-pitched squeals punctuated the fact that sometimes complete days passed when I didn't use my brain for anything more challenging than inserting another disk into the DVD player.

All the questions about being a police officer brought me to the same place. Did I want this particular job, or did I want moments in my life that would allow me—because of their violence and immediacy—to forget I was a mother? This was the question I didn't have an answer to. Its very existence was shameful. Every man I knew went to work and forgot about his kids. Husbands were unreachable during emergencies. Part of me imagined that being a police officer would be like this—I could be a dad instead of a mom. I could outsource the difficult. Someone else could run in the sleet with Gus and Grace. Then I recognized my fantasy, that I was dreaming, populating my present with past freedoms. I would always track my children in real time. It was 9:30 a.m. on a rainy Saturday in April. Gus and Grace would be finished with their race now, hair wet and stringy.

"When was the last time you dressed to impress someone?" Dr. Rosenberger asked.

"This morning." I stretched a creased pantleg beneath my chair.

She nodded and continued. "When was the last time you felt out of your element or lacking confidence?"

"Yesterday. I got pulled over in my husband's car for a broken taillight and no inspection sticker." The rain had stopped, leaving behind an expectant steam, a relentless drip, as if nature were colluding with Dr. Rosenberger to wring the world dry.

"Why did that make you feel out of your element?" Dr. Rosenberger asked.

"It took me by surprise and scared me." Dr. Rosenberger jotted something on her legal pad.

"If you could change anything about yourself, what would it be?"

"Sometimes I think it would be easier if I didn't see the world in moral absolutes. My friend stayed with her cheating husband. That's not me. You make a commitment to fidelity. We get to do this once. Life isn't a test you get to retake."

Dr. Rosenberger kept her pencil still, poised above her papers. "What's the closest you've come to breaking the law?"

"In high school, a group of about twenty of us rented a hotel room on Market Street and drank all night." The Penn Center Inn had been demolished twenty years ago, but the memories of a night spent on a hotel carpet, next to cans of dip, lasted forever.

"Is there something more recent?" she asked.

"Not that that comes to mind."

She tapped my file. "What about this pot and the mushrooms in 1988?"

"Oh, right. That."

"Yes. That." Drip. Bang. Drip. The wind kicked the shade against the window frame and water spilled out of clogged gutters.

"That's not really on my radar," I said, distracted by the duet of wind and rain. "I'm healthy. I don't do drugs. I run a lot."

"Those things were a crime. Pot wasn't legal in 1988." We sat in a long silence, listening to the storm leave the city, before she continued. "If you could change anything about your personality, what would it be?"

"I'd be younger."

"That's not part of your personality." Now was not the time for a philosophical discussion, but I knew differently. I'd do anything to remove the NICU and all the other hospitals, to excise two years from my memory and become forty-five again. Forty-five without the fear.

"Well," Dr. Rosenberger shuffled papers on her desk. "We're finished here. Do you have any questions for me before you leave?"

"Why does the Philadelphia Police Department use the MMPI instead of the Myers-Briggs Personality Test?" The test to determine my sanity had taken less than an hour. If I hurried, I could beat Augie home.

"It's better for the department." Dr. Rosenberger pushed the button to stop recording. "Anything else?"

"How did I do on the MMPI?"

"I saw no anomalies." She didn't look at her notes.

"How did I do today?"

Dr. Rosenberger sat back as if I'd just asked her to hand me her ATM card. "I can't tell you that. I need to process the whole interview. How do you think you did?"

I snorted. Welcome back to therapy. "I'm the person I am," I said. "That's all I can be." She waited for me to say something more, something damning. Instead, I offered my hand, "Thank you."

"The department will be in touch."

On the drive home from the precinct office, rain glazed the streets. Clouds shifted, a kaleidoscope of dark winter and cumulus spring. Inside our house, wet clothes were everywhere. I picked up one muddy sock, then another, following the breadcrumb trail to the master bath. Shrieks of laughter hit me. One hand on the doorknob, I wondered if I'd made a deal with the devil. As I neared the end of the police department's hiring process, had I dedicated myself to missing Gus's and Grace's childhood? Maybe this, here, was the definition of insanity.

I pushed the door open. Augie sat in the middle of the Jacuzzi tub, fully dressed. Bubble bath peaks surrounded him. "We were cold," he said.

"Yeah." I pointed to the pile of soaking clothes in my hand. "I'm getting that."

"Hi Mommy!" Gus popped up from behind the island that was Augie. With both doors closed, the bathroom air was thick, almost Jurassic.

"Look, Mommy," Grace said, her ears covered with a mop cap of bubbles. "I turned into Martha Washington while you were gone."

"How was the test?" Augie asked.

"Fine." I cupped my hands behind my neck and rolled my head. "Tough. I don't know. Fun? The closest I've come to an interview in this whole process." I sat on the toilet across from the tub. "How was the race?"

"There was a huge hill," Augie said. "We had to walk a little, didn't we, guys?" Busy sticking their little otter paws into each other's ears and hair, Gus and Grace said nothing. Augie shook his head, apologizing for their behavior.

"It doesn't matter," I said. "They can tell me later." Just like that, the experience was gone. Augie could describe the race. I could buy the pictures, but it would always be something I'd missed. "Can we turn the water off?" I reached for the faucet and shrugged out of my suit jacket. "It's a sauna in here."

"Mommy, make me into a burrito," Grace demanded. I grabbed a towel and scooped her up.

"Yummy." I turned so Grace's feet hung over the tub. Gus stood with a shiver. "Gus, this is the part where the beans are." I pushed Grace toward him. "Take a bite."

"No, Mommy, no!" Grace shouted, scissoring her legs. A corner of the towel dragged through the water.

"There's a child in here, Mommy." Augie reached over to re-wrap Grace. "Not rice and beans."

"Oh, no," I said. "And here I was, ravenous." Grace giggled. No matter how many times we played this game, Gus and Grace always laughed.

"Hey, beautiful girl." I kissed Grace's forehead. Against the dark tile floor, her eyes were a luminous iceberg blue. "I'm glad you didn't disappear on us." A small smile played on the side of her mouth. She reached up and pulled my ponytail free of its elastic.

"Do the other game, Mommy."

"Get ready for the suds." My hair fell in a curtain. "Car wash." Head swinging, my hair swished up and down her body, tickling her.

"Again."

"Uh, no." I shook a finger at her. "You only paid for one car wash."

"But Mommm—"

"Show us the tub," Gus interrupted Grace. "And tell us the story."

"Augie, did you ever do that survival floating test as a life-guard?" I piled wet clothes on the side of the tub.

"The one where you make your clothes into a life-preserver, but it never works and you sit there sinking for ninety minutes?"

"Yeah—"

"Tell us the story," Gus repeated. Augie opened the cabinet and handed me a pink plastic tub. Measuring 12 by 8 inches, it was the only object left from the NICU.

"There isn't really a story," I said. "We bathed you guys in this for the first six months."

"That's not a very good story."

"Hmmm." I considered my daughter, my head tilted, thinking about the nature of stories. "How about the one where you got the potty stuck on your head?"

"Yes, yes, yes." Gus clapped.

"Well, one day—"

"No, Mommy, no." Grace kicked the wall in protest.

"Grace decided to put her head through the potty." I raised my voice. "Not the poopy bowl part. The other part. And we could not get that thing off. We tried Vaseline—"

"The saw?" Gus asked.

"Maybe not the saw." Cold steam had settled on the walls, streaking it with tear drops. "Nothing worked. We had to strap her and her toilet into the car seat and drive to the fire department and explain that our daughter is not so, um, bright."

"Mommy," Grace threatened. "You take that back. Right now."

"I'm just teasing you, honey."

"Say it's a bad story." The last of the water drained out of the tub with a slurp.

"It's a very, very bad story," I said.

Grace frowned. "I don't accept your apology."

"I don't remember apologizing."

"How about a game of Tickle Monster then?" Augie lurched toward us, zombie arms outstretched. Both kids vaulted away, their cherub bums disappearing around corners, only to return to taunt us, wavering just out of reach.

"Gotcha!" I tackled Gus, and we sat on the heated bathroom floor. Watery footprints and scoops of bubble bath evaporated around us, reminding me that someday soon Gus and Grace would become too old for tickles and stories. This, this rapidly disappearing present, was the deal with the devil I'd made when I applied to the PPD. When would we play this game for the last time? Would we mark its passing? My neighbor Maggie kept an endless list of her children's firsts. The first time her daughter jumped into the pool without water wings. The first time her boys accompanied her into the voting booth.

Gus spread his arms wide. "Do you know how much I love you, Mommy?"

"How much?"

"More than you can even imagine." He peeked up for a moment before resting his head against me. Where Grace had solemn eyes of Izmir-blue, Gus's were gray with yellow tints ringed by dark lashes. Cat's eyes.

"Not as much as I love you."

"More Tickle Monster," he demanded. Just like that, the moment was gone.

As Gus ran in circles, I returned to Maggie's first moments. They were a way of hedging life against loss, of believing you could collect enough memories to build an insulating wall around yourself. Maggie's brother and father had died, young and unexpectedly. She kept a stranglehold on the present. Her list created a world that was always marching forward, always joyful, a world of beginnings with no room for tragedy.

In the weeks after the psychological evaluation, my words to Dr. Rosenberger—that we got to do this once—stayed with me, making me pull my children close. My phone pinged in Acme where Gus and Grace were fighting over who got to drive the firetruck grocery cart.

Megan,

Call me when you get this message.

Det. Brody

I threw items into the basket, racing through aisles filled with the smell of wet cardboard and the loneliness of single-serve frozen pizza. Once home, I unpacked the groceries and returned the detective's call.

"I have some bad news for you," Detective Brody said. No hello. No nothing.

"Okay." Rummaging through the last bag, I discovered a four-pound container of chocolate chips, carefully hidden beneath the carrots. Definitely Grace's handiwork.

"After May 9th," Detective Brody continued, "you won't be working as a coach anymore."

"What?" I pushed a pile of mail across the counter. Summer camp schedules. Enrichment programs. Bed Bath & Beyond coupons.

"Congratulations! You've been accepted into the academy."

Still holding the last bag, I stumbled outside. Mia followed me, banging the back door open. "May 9th? As in next week?" I sat on the damp stoop. In the flower bed next to me, the Lenten rose poked curled green fingers through the dirt, reaching for summer. "But I have another job."

"So, you need to give two weeks' notice?" he asked. "You could do the June class?"

"No, I committed to an editing job in August." At my feet, Mia cocked her head and lowered herself into sphinx position, her broad shoulders dappled in the light.

"That's going to be a problem," the detective said. "You do understand that the police academy is a full-time adult commitment?"

"Yes, I understand that." I paused to pull the phone from my ear and give it the finger. This I needed. A lecture from a man ten years my junior about what it meant to be an adult. "Detective Brody. You need to understand this from my perspective," I continued. "I've been applying to this job for more than eighteen months." Breathe. Flowers. Spring. "Eighteen months," I repeated. "A year and a half. You expect me to drop everything in a week. I can't do that. No adult could." Concerned, Mia rose and head-butted me.

As I was facedown in the mud, Detective Brody kept talking. "I understand, I understand. It's not me. It's the city. The class after that should start sometime in September."

"September would work." I picked up my phone.

"Great. I need you to come in on Monday and sign a declaration."

"A declaration?" A smear of dirt covered my phone screen.

"A declaration of declination."

"You can't just make a note that I'm deferring?" I rubbed my phone clean against my jeans.

"Nope."

"You want me to come to your office on Monday, May 9th, five days from now?"

"Yeah," he laughed.

I wanted to ask him *who's on first?* but didn't. In true Philadelphia Police Department fashion, we ended the conversation exactly where we'd begun.

★ ★ ★

The weather was balmy when I returned to the recruiting center. The whole world was outside, and a soft green coating of new grass covered the empty lots along Wissahickon Avenue. Delivery trucks clogged the sidewalk, making me sidestep into an open storefront. The garage smelled like gerbils. Pine shavings clung to my newly-polished shoes. The store was a funeral supply store. The police and fire stations were next to a casket maker. Not great marketing.

In his cubicle, Detective Brody was chattier than he'd ever been. "We don't have a start date for you yet," he said, smoothing the brown triangles on his tie. "Should be sometime in September."

"When will you know exactly? I need to arrange child care."

"I'll let you know the minute I do. Meanwhile, call Angel at the beginning of August to schedule your physical."

"What?"

"Your drug test is only valid for six months."

"You mean I have to go back to Nineteenth and Fairmount?"

"'Fraid so." He grinned. Across the aisle, Detective MacDonald swiveled his chair and laughed.

"Crap. I've had whole days swallowed by that place," I said. "What days off in the fall do we get?"

"You don't get days off," MacDonald said.

"Not even Thanksgiving or Christmas?"

"Oh, those," Detective Brody said. "Yeah, you get those off, and New Year's."

"That's it?"

"This is a full-time job." MacDonald gestured to the half-filled room of cubicles. "You don't even get the day after Thanksgiving off. No shopping."

"Ha. Good one, Bob." Detective Brody turned back to me. "You sure you don't want to start today?"

"I wish. I'm trapped at home with the kids all summer." It was only May, but the air already held the heaviness of August. The pool would open in three weeks, and soon my days would be filled with sunburns, soggy French fries, and chlorine.

CHAPTER TEN

BROKEN BONES AND PYGMY DONKEYS

JUNE 2016
SUBURBAN PHILADELPHIA

BY THE SECOND WEEK OF JUNE, the weather was already so sweltering, the very concept of summer felt oppressive. I parked beneath a giant walnut tree at Abington Friends School and walked Gus and Grace across the parking lot for the last time as second graders. The mixture of sadness and happiness that accompanied every school year's end engulfed me. I breathed in the soupy air and counted. Based on the estimated start date Detective Brody had given me, I had ten weeks before the academy.

For a kid, the last day of school dawned brilliantly, eclipsing even Christmas in magnitude. It was Christmas without the letdown. The next day arrived with the same sense of promise. And the day after. Until August, when dread appeared. In my memory, it never rained on the last day of school. The sun rose, brighter than it had been all spring. Tamsen and I ate our English muffins, our legs swinging beneath the stools, fidgeting in the face of a beckoning freedom. Dismissal was at noon, four long hours away.

In the classroom, the ugly black-and-white face of the sixties-era clock ticked with the backwards regularity of a metronome. My bike was rusty from a winter spent indoors. My bathing suit still in its package. I couldn't wait to get home, to take off my sneakers and socks, to wince and hop as my naked winter feet hit the ground for the first time.

In the seventies of my childhood, summer was the sound of slamming screen doors as my sister and I sprinted outside, under our sprinkler, through the neighbor's yard. Neighborhood houses were porous then—my sister and I thought nothing of racing through the Ciolfi's house and stopping for lunch. I knew that kitchen like my own, its yellow vinyl countertop pockmarked from where Mrs. Ciolfi cut the edges off our Wonder Bread sandwiches. Summer days were tactile, eternally present. We were eight and five, full of a barefoot freedom, but we were learned in the differences between houses. Mrs. Salzman's huge kitchen smelled of furniture polish and Kraft macaroni. The Slobodian's second-floor twin apartment stank of minced meat and cabbage.

All summer we charged around on bikes, bikini-clad and helmetless, ignoring our mothers. The neighborhood was its own country. Plains animals migrating toward watering holes, the kids knew all the shortcuts, the single-track paths that led directly to our best friends' houses. A rounded brown storage mailbox squatted on the corner of Orchard and Robbins Streets, a natural pausing point to catch our breaths after running through Mr. Arizmendi's flower beds. We waited there for him to roar out his front door, waving his cane. On the days he didn't, we unraveled a hose and covered the mailbox with water. It was too hot and too easy to climb dry. We lined up and leaped at the brown box, wildebeest scrambling on all fours.

"Why did we just go to the Five and Ten to buy you Dr. Scholl's?" my mother complained, the wooden slap of her clogs on our ceramic floor as much the sound of summer as the screen doors we banged. Before my mother began working in business, we didn't have money to waste on shoes we didn't wear. On display next to the bare bum of the Coppertone ad, the Dr. Scholl's were grown-up shoes. But when I wore them, the leather straps bit into the soft tops of my feet, leaving a stinging badge of summer.

"Put on your shoes," my mom said as my sister and I galloped around the dining room table, sprinkler mud caked between our toes. "And for the last time," she yelled as we picked up our bikes and coasted down the block to Frank's penny store on Commonwealth Avenue, "turn off the sprinkler."

My mother was home the summer I was eight and my sister five. She was a constant presence, coloring the edges of our enjoyment. There, but peripheral. Helping us crack open the homemade orange juice popsicles that overflowed onto the freezer floor or coating herself with baby oil in the backyard. More body than anything, she was the voice tethering us home with shouts of "Dinner!" The hands that pushed us outside in the morning with an exasperated, "Just. Go. Play!" Childhood was different now. There were no wooden screen doors, no porous houses. I couldn't shove my children outside and forget about them.

My mother hovered on the borders of summer, always there. And we knew it. In the maze of grazing paths that defined the neighborhood, there was a beeline straight to her when someone scraped a knee or fell from a tree. We couldn't afford air conditioning, and the slap of the sprinkler cooled our house during the day. At dusk, the hot summer air rose to our second-floor bedrooms. My mother coated us with witch hazel. For a brief moment before bed, we shivered, breathing the astringent smell before it evaporated and we dozed off to sleep, fans whirring in the background.

★ ★ ★

As I walked beneath the canopy that surrounded Abington Friends School, I was struck by how different the end of the school year was as a parent. My children itchy with excitement, I was leaving something behind. After this day, Gus and Grace would never again be second graders. They knew how to read, to add and subtract. Only yesterday each had weighed less than three pounds, dwarfed by a tub too small for dishes.

School that morning was a zoo, with cars zipping around us. "Give me your hands."

"No hands, Mommy," Gus said.

"No hands? What are we, biking?" From the moment Gus got his first training wheels, he was determined to bike without hands, even if his feet couldn't reach the pedals.

"No, Mommy." Gus's face was firm as he held both hands away from me, surrounded by students chattering and treading time before summer vacation. "I'm a big kid now. I walk alone." And just like that, with the simple declarative sentences of an eight-year-old, everything slowed. There was only this moment, filled with a grief so overflowing my hands couldn't wrap around it. All I could do was shrug and keep walking, clutching Grace's hand a little bit tighter.

"I hope the kids will be okay with a nanny when I go back to work," I said when I picked my mother up at the train station later that day. She'd arrived to help paint my hallway—the latest in a long list of projects to avoid sitting at my computer and trying to write. In the five years we'd lived in Philadelphia, I'd renovated the basement, painted the exterior of the house, wallpapered three rooms, and painted all the ceilings. I was now about to have stenciled Indian elephants and yellow stripes in my mudroom.

"Your kids are old enough now for you to leave them." My mom brushed my fears away. With a swish of her hand, my contribution to Gus and Grace's childhood was erased. It was ninety degrees, but my mother wore her eternal lime green cashmere pantsuit. So much privilege and drive were wrapped in that pantsuit: a PhD from Harvard, an MBA, growing up in Shaker Heights, the daughter of the head of Internal Medicine at the Cleveland

Clinic. She wore that outfit to Puerto Rico when she whisked me and Tamsen away as a surprise for my thirtieth birthday. She wore it when she flew to volunteer in India and Bangladesh. The year it hit ninety-five degrees during the Boston Marathon, Augie and I were watching the race from our couch in San Francisco when the camera focused on the crowd lining Heartbreak Hill.

"Wait a second. Is that—?" Augie leaned forward.

"Jesus Christ." I rewound the DVR. There, indeed, was my mother. Surrounded by puking runners, she was leaning against a tree in her signature lime green cashmere pantsuit.

I did not share my mother's certainty that my kids would survive without me. I pictured Gus's arm when he'd broken it three weeks before. The kids had been playing in the basement with friends. I was in the kitchen. Beneath me, bodies thumped and hinges creaked. These were normal sounds. Then I heard a shriek that made me drop everything and run. As a parent, you knew that sound.

"My arm is broken, Mommy," Gus howled from the bottom of the stairs. "Mommy, help."

"You're going to be all right, honey." I jumped down the stairs. "You didn't break anything." Sobbing, he lifted his little white arm, a puppy holding his paw for me to fix. Twisted like an S, his arm no longer belonged to him. It was now a gelatinous thing, without fibers.

"So, yeah," I told him, rubbing his back and pushing him upstairs. "We're going to the hospital *right now.*"

"Mommymommymommy," he hyperventilated in one long word. "Are they going to cut me open?"

"No, honey." Calming words came out of my mouth, but I couldn't breathe. Time froze. My neighbor Hilary came to watch Grace and her friends. I went upstairs three times. Each time, I circled, dazed, forgetting I was there for my wallet and insurance card. The three girls stood in the hall, their eyes flicking back and forth between me and Gus. "Go upstairs. Go upstairs and play." They didn't need to see this. I didn't need to see this.

"Mommy," Grace said, wobbling on the edge of tears. "Gus's arm doesn't look like an arm anymore."

"Upstairs," I pointed.

"What if they can't fix my arm?" Gus asked.

"Don't be silly, Goose." I flicked his nose, as if this were all one big joke. "If doctors can fix Mommy, they can fix you." He nodded. Normally, my skewed logic wouldn't make it past his honey-badger brain.

"Sit still, hon. I'm going to wrap your arm to protect it for the car ride." Too bent to be splinted, I couldn't bear to look. Gus and Grace had had their share of illnesses, stitches, hospital stays. Nothing had prepared me for this moment. Gus's misshapen arm, so quickly bowed, made me realize how perfect my children were, how ungrateful I'd been for their straight limbs and everyday gestures.

Somehow, I drove us to the hospital, cars and traffic signals swimming around me. Gus was uncharacteristically wordless, his snuffling sobs our only soundtrack. Parked sideways in the Emergency Room lot, I opened Gus's door.

"Take them, take them." I threw my keys at the attendants and scooped Gus into my arms.

"I can walk," Gus said again. "Don't pick me up, Mommy."

My hands cupped my temples, making an imaginary vise. "Can you not do this independence thing right now, Gus? You just broke your arm." More than anything, I needed to hold him, to bury my head against him, to believe that somewhere beneath all that hair I could still smell my glabrous newborn.

Inside Abington Memorial, the triage nurse pressed the button to unseal the doors. In an instant, nurses swarmed, taking Gus's temperature, his weight, his pulse oxygen level. Several policemen huddled in the corner, idly sipping coffee and joking with the nurses. One of them bent to Gus's height.

"Why the long face, buddy?" he asked. "You don't look very sick." Gus looked from his arm to me in confusion. In an instant, my fear transformed into something white hot.

"His arm is fucking broken, you moron."

"Oh, Jesus." The officer blanched. "Um, sorry?"

A nurse pushed a wheelchair into the room. It was unclear whether it was for me or for Gus. Standing before the police and the nurses, I was stripped of all veneer, feral in my desire to protect my son.

After triage, things proceeded quickly. X-rays, the orthopedist, the attending, then the IV for pain. "I'm just going to thread a straw into your arm for medicine," a nurse past her expiration date explained to Gus.

"No."

"What do you mean, 'no'?" She stopped untangling tubing.

"N-O." Gus spelled the word out. "That sounds horrible." The nurse scowled. I raised my eyebrows. On this one, I was going to have to side with my son. If someone said they wanted to stick a straw into my veins, I'd run like hell. "I want my mom to do it." Gus crossed his one good arm across his chest. "Not you."

"Uh, Gus?" I started laughing. "That won't turn out so well for you."

"You're a doctor," he said.

"Not that kind of doctor—"

"If your mom does it," the nurse interrupted, "blood will spurt all over this room and drip down the wall in puddles."

Stepping between my son and the nurse, I touched her arm. "I think we're done here."

"I still need to start his IV," she said, stretching the rubber tourniquet.

"No. You don't. Another nurse will be starting his IV."

"I can do it," she said.

"I'm not letting someone put an IV in my son's arm who just talked about the room filling with blood. Get me another nurse." She turned and left, white Crocs squishing on the linoleum.

"Next time we're going to Children's," I told Gus. "It's fucking amateur hour here."

"Mommy, you swore."

"Yeah, sometimes there are days when you just need to fucking swear."

"That nurse really sucked." We fist-pumped, fingers snaking in our own private handshake.

"Looks like I'm starting your IV, kid." Dr. Xavier the orthopedist, arrived with a whoosh. In a matter of minutes, Gus's eyelashes fluttered. "Do you want me to explain what we're going to do here?" he asked.

"Um? Yeah."

"We're going to give him Ketamine. It's been proven to be very effective for kids his age."

"A veterinary drug?"

"Yes. I'll set the radius and ulna, then X-ray." Dr. Xavier was talking to everyone in the room but me. He was over-tanned, fit, maybe twelve years old. "If everything looks good, I'll cast it, and you can be on your way. At this age, the bones are more like starfish than bones. Flexible."

"Will he feel anything?"

"He won't remember feeling anything." He unwrapped bandages and positioned his tray.

"Hold on, hold on." I stepped forward. "Go back to that part about memory."

"He won't remember the pain."

"Not remembering pain is not the same as not feeling it."

"True," Dr. Xavier said. Lights hummed above us, filling the spaces between his words with yellow fluorescence. "We've found this is the safest drug for kids his age," he added after a long silence. "Almost zero risk of complication. Ready?" he asked the team.

Everyone except me nodded. He put two hands on Gus's forearm and twisted. Gus's eyes popped open. He screamed a scream unlike anything I'd ever heard. And he didn't stop.

"Mommy, mommy, mommy, help me!" he pleaded, trying to sit up and move toward me while two orderlies held him down.

"You might want to sit." The attending held out a supporting hand.

"I'm not going to faint." I pushed him away. "What I might do is jump across this gurney and rip your throat out."

"I'm done." The orthopedist stepped back. "Let's do the X-ray."

"Hi, Gus." The X-ray technician slipped the plate beneath Gus's arm. "I'm Bob."

Gus's eyes were doe-large in their terror, following me in wobbles. "Hi, Bob," a small voice whispered.

"I thought you said he'd be asleep."

"He won't remember anything," Dr. Xavier said.

"That was just about the worst thing I've ever experienced as a parent." My words came out in waves, foaming with anger and helplessness. "Ever. I'm never, ever, going to get over this."

Dr. Xavier nodded. "That's how it usually goes."

"I don't care how it 'usually goes.' That sucked."

Dr. Xavier scanned the films. "These look good. Let's cast it." After Gus's arm was wrapped, we waited for an hour for the medication to wear off. Left alone in the room, I slid onto the bed next to Gus and deflated. Aftershocks shuddered through me. I had nothing left. No air. No breath. No fight. The day had taken almost everything I had. An hour later, I hoisted Gus around my midsection like a baby orangutan, his head lolling softly against my shoulder.

"Hi, Bob!" Gus waved to the X-ray technician in the hall.

"Hi, uh, Gus," Bob mumbled. We paused together for a loaded moment. Gus should not have remembered the X-ray technician's name. I walked out the door, drowning in the full extent of my failure. Not only had my son broken his arm on my watch, he'd had two bones set without anesthesia.

For the next month, Gus had a cast up to his shoulder. He was eight years old. It was summer, and he couldn't run. Unable to brace his fall, he might break the other arm. He lurched around the house all day, a one-armed zombie. At night, the screaming returned.

"Mommy, mommy, do something!" Gus pleaded. Even in my dreams, I was paralyzed, holding his hand, unable to act.

"It's not as if your kids are infants, anymore," my mother repeated on the last day of school. "They will be fine when you start the academy. They don't need you the way they used to." While her words might have been true, I pictured Gus's arm, how his eyes had popped open, searching for me. At least I'd been there. I'd been present. If there was an accident when I went back to work, someone else would hold my child's hand at the hospital. The academy didn't allow cell phones. I thought of the deer tracks through my childhood neighborhood, how quickly we galloped home when we were afraid. About how my mom gave me witch hazel at night when I was hot and warm ginger ale when I was sick. However old we were, we never outgrew our primal scream, our need for our mothers.

"It's time for you to be something besides a mom," my mother said. She was strident, so determined in what she wanted for me that I no longer felt the ginger ale and witch hazel in her voice.

"Is that even possible?" Breakfast on the last day of school had been filled with yelling, curdled milk, and the demands of eight-year-olds.

Gus had delivered one final ultimatum at his classroom door that morning. "If you really loved me, you'd buy me a pygmy donkey."

"Great," I said. "We will name your donkey 'Snack,' for when Mia and Shady eat it."

"You're the meanest mommy *ever.*"

"Right." I inhaled, tasting the lower-school smell of melted crayons and Elmer's glue sticks. I might be a bad mother, but I also knew there were exactly two pygmy donkeys for rescue in our tri-state area.

"You've a very narrow window to get back in the workforce, Megan," my mother said as she unrolled blue painter's tape. "You don't want to turn fifty with nothing to show for yourself besides being a mom. You're too educated and too ambitious."

I tested my brush on newspaper, where it left a streak of water and hardened paint chips. "Do you think we should go back to using oil-based paint?"

"No." My mother shook her head. "We'd have to buy all new brushes. Oil and water, you know."

"We might need to buy new ones anyway. I did a crappy job cleaning these." Gunk clogged my bristles.

"You never know," my mother continued, bobbed hair brushing against her cashmere turtleneck. "It might be good for Gus and Grace to spend some time away from you." Her words decimated me. I couldn't imagine a world where I didn't need her, or my children didn't need me. For eight years, I'd covered their cuts with SpongeBob Band-Aids and woken when they cried. The idea that they might not need me opened an abyss, an unfathomable absence of self-definition.

"Your children could stand to grow up a bit," my mom added, the final nail in my coffin. I slid straight down her words into my thirteenth summer. I was at the dinner table with my parents. It was winter in Watertown. Storm windows stood between my family and the fossilized landscape of a New England winter. "I've signed you up for a summer program in France," my mother declared over lamb chops and mint jelly. "I'm hoping it will make you less shy."

"I don't want to go to France." I dropped my fork.

"Of course you want to go to France," she corrected, fingering her eighties silk bow. An hour before cooking dinner, she'd been an investment banker. "Everyone wants to go to France."

"No. I really don't," I said, while my father hid behind his lamb chop. "I want to stay in Watertown. You want me to go to France."

"You're right. It's time you became more independent."

"What's wrong with me the way I am?" I threw my napkin across my plate and ran upstairs, propelled by the righteous indignation of a thirteen-year-old girl. My mother never answered me. Not then, not today. I went to France that summer, and then to boarding school a year later.

Not until Gus dropped my hand on the last day of school did I learn that need could be something you outgrew, instead of a shameful feeling that should be cut to the quick, cauterized like the forced separations of my own childhood. Gus was just growing up. Naturally.

Staring down the barrel of my last summer at home with Gus and Grace, the awareness that in the fall a nanny would pick them up at school—would be the first to hear about their day—repelled me. This was a familiar feeling, one I recognized from my first days as a parent when friends suggested childcare options. One moment in particular stands out in my memory. I was five months pregnant. Augie and I were with our friends, Jon and Jodi, in the Presidio, the heat of a wood-burning oven mixing with the salt of the San Francisco Bay.

"If your twins are born early," Jodi advised, "you're going to want a night nanny."

"What the hell is a night nanny?" Augie asked, suspicious of anything that cost money.

"Someone who comes from ten to six every night so you can sleep." Jon said this as if it were the most natural thing in the world to have a stranger stay in your house and take care of your newborns. "Best money you'll ever spend," Jodi added. "Even if it's a small fortune."

"How much?" Augie asked.

"A semester of college tuition." Jodi waved her hand in the air, putting their past where it belonged. "Maybe twenty thousand dollars?"

"I want to take care of my kids myself." I rubbed my belly. Augie nodded, his cheeks red from our walk to dinner. The sun had only just started to set when we'd left our house, painting the windows on Broderick Street a golden enamel, then disappearing beneath the eucalyptus trees.

"So," Jodi spoke slowly. "Your kids will probably be born early. They'll wake up every two hours. Maybe for a year. Maybe longer. It won't be the same two hours. You'll only have just finished with one when the other will need to be fed, changed, burped. The whole nine yards."

"You'll be up all night, every night," Jon said, his ironed pink gingham shirt contradicting the chaos of his words. "You'll be so tired, you'll forget your children's names."

"Funny," I said, but they weren't joking.

"I do pretty well with sleep deprivation," Augie offered.

"You have no idea." Jodi shut him down. "Just set something up. You can always cancel."

That was how I came to be standing in my kitchen in Pacific Heights at 3 a.m., wanting to kill a woman because she was holding Grace. The kids had been home together for two weeks, during which time Augie and I had sleep-walked through nighttime feedings. It was Sunday. Augie returned to work the next day, and we were starting a trial week with Nicole, the night nanny.

In the still hours of early morning, Grace's newborn cry propelled me out of bed. "They're up." I shoved Augie awake. In an instant, I was fully alert, making a beeline for the twins' bedroom.

"Night nanny," Augie mumbled. Faced with Grace's empty crib, I backtracked to the kitchen, searching for my daughter. She was ensconced in Nicole's arms, guzzling a bottle. It took everything I had not to flatten Nicole, to wrestle Grace from her arms. Never before had I felt this primal possessiveness, this visceral certainty that another person belonged to me.

"She's mine," I wanted to whisper, my head rotating like Linda Blair's.

"Everything okay?" Nicole raised an eyebrow.

"Yeah, yeah. I just heard Grace cry. I need to pump."

"Then go back to sleep," Nicole said. "Let me do my job."

Picking up the cold silicon cups of my breast pump, I promised myself that in the morning I'd fire Nicole. As it turned out, Nicole ended up working for us for five months. Even with her help, my exhaustion was catatonic. As Jodi had promised, I forgot my children's names. At the end-of-the-year party, when I was drowning in final papers, sleeping on my father's floor with the twins as I renovated our kitchen so we could sell our condo, my colleague Roseanne asked politely, "Who's your son named after?" I had three classes to teach the next day, but I couldn't track this conversation. "Your son?" Roseanne prompted. "August? It's an unusual name?"

"Yes, yes, it is." My brain was frozen fingers, trying to grasp the key to her question. This question was not difficult. All that came up was blanks, fumbles. "I have no idea," I said.

"Get some sleep." Roseanne patted my back.

★　★　★

As I looked ahead to my last summer at home with my children, I often returned to my memories of the early days of motherhood. In eight years, my desire to be their primary caregiver hadn't changed but my stamina had. I knew a different exhaustion now—the chipping away of reserves that happened in the wake of more tantrums and emergency room visits than I could count.

The first days and then weeks of summer passed, startling in their shimmering heat. We'd transitioned almost immediately from the forced-air claustrophobia of winter to the muggy stillness of August. All Gus and Grace did was swim. I spent hours poolside, a naked mole rat squinting beneath my coverup. Their summer was different from those of my childhood. Here, in Philadelphia, we locked our doors. There was no witch hazel, no fans, no Dr. Scholl's. On the rare moments when we were at home and the weather exceeded 100 degrees, we hermetically sealed the house closed. The clean smell of chlorine permeated everything, even our sheets. In my childhood, we were always hot, dirty, sweaty. My family couldn't afford pool membership, so Tamsen and I would sit for hours on the top of our swing set, staring over the fence at the Ciolfis, who were chest-deep in water, the blue skin of their above-ground pool wrinkling around them as they splashed.

Summer became mid-August, and still I refused to hire a nanny, even though Detective Brody could call any day. Ambivalence combined with sunburned days to breed apathy. It was an impossible dilemma—I wanted to go back to work, but I didn't want someone else to take care of my children. I wanted a career outside the home because my children drove me crazy. I knew that working made me a better mother. When I finally started my nanny search, I scrolled through entry after entry of energetic college students with excitement. As a mom, I yelled. A lot. If McDonald's had served fries and nuggets for breakfast, we'd eat three meals a day there. I criticized my kids for accidental mistakes. Now, I could hire someone who was better at this than I. Someone who wouldn't swear when Gus melted down, for the third time in a week, because I refused to buy him a pygmy donkey.

Our nanny would be a better me. The mother I could be if I didn't have to live with my children. I emailed bubbly candidate after candidate. None of them responded. Weeks after I first reached out, one replied breezily. "Sorry, I've been down the shore for the week." More often than not, I was the victim of the single emoticon text message, or worse, "Call me if you want to talk!" Drowning in smiley faces, I hated this generation of college students. The women who responded immediately to my ad were older, their children grown.

With three weeks left in the summer, I decided to meet Martha, one of the grandmotherly types, at Build-A-Bagel in Jenkintown. I arrived early and ordered a latte. The day was turning into a scorcher. A slow river of sweat ran down my arms and pooled at my elbows. Dog drool covered my shorts. My shirt had a huge stain under the right boob, as if I were lactating jam.

An unremarkable Ford Focus eased into the lot. The driver picked her way gingerly into the coffee shop. This could not be Martha. While this woman looked lovely, exuding an almost subliminal smell of home-baked cookies and snuggles, she was too old. Too slow. Too fragile.

"Martha?" I tried to drain the despair from my voice.

"Megan?" She tilted her head sideways before hugging me. Her bag knocked against my stomach. It was a quilted elephant, her wallet a stuffed giraffe. Everything about Martha was padded and soothing. My children would break her.

We chose to sit beneath an umbrella instead of shivering inside. "I can sit in the sun," I told Martha. She was pasty white, her face elfin in its intensity. "Tell me about yourself."

"Well," Martha smiled. "I have four boys."

"Wait, what?" Nowhere in her application had I seen signs of the post-apocalyptic exhaustion that must accompany raising four boys.

"Yes." She wrapped a world of pride into that single word.

"How old?"

"Twenty-seven, twenty-five, twenty-three, and nineteen." She leaned back, her body living proof of the accomplishment. "There's nothing your kids can hit me with that I haven't already experienced. Stitches, broken bones, birth control. You name it, I've seen it."

"Gus broke his arm in the beginning of the summer. It was one of the worst moments of my life."

Martha touched my forearm. "Did the bone come through the skin?"

"No, thank God." Rain had swept into Philadelphia overnight, a sudden violent downpour that I'd listened to, awake with my nightmares at 3 a.m. Now, the parking lot shimmered, cooler puddles evaporating into steam. "I was completely nonfunctional. As if I were moving through cement."

"I know that feeling." The sun was climbing quickly across the sky, making Martha squint.

"Are you getting burned?" I asked. "Let's switch chairs." We moved, beginning a dance around the metal table that lasted for the next ninety minutes.

"Thanks." She rubbed freckled hands. "Good that the bone didn't come through the skin. That happened to my son. I get it.

You do what you have to. You go to the hospital. Muscle through the panic."

"Exactly. Hopefully, you won't have to deal with any broken bones—"

"Hopefully not. But my four are living proof that I can."

"And Gus and Grace are eight. They still take baths together. No conversations about birth control needed."

"That," she squiggled her eyebrows, "was one of *my* worst parenting moments." The rungs of my chair dug into my back as I waited for the tangent, for the story. Although I'd only just met her, I'd learned these sideways conversations were part of Martha's very fabric. "I got home from work early one day," Martha rubbed her eyes, preparing to cross-stitch a story for me. "And I heard my son having sex in his room."

"Oh, God." This was about as far from my current conception of motherhood as you could get. "How old was he?"

"I dunno. It was so long ago. Now, let me think." She paused, pulling the answer into the present. "Maybe sixteen?"

"Okay."

"I didn't care he was having sex. I was worried he was having unprotected sex. I marched to his room, flung open the door, and yelled, 'Show me the condom!'"

I spit out my latte. "You did not."

"Oh, yes, I did."

"Wow." I mopped my chin. "Just wow."

"In retrospect," she circled back a bit. "I might have gone overboard. Ever since they were ten years old, I'd told my boys to use condoms. I absolutely was not having a teenage pregnancy in my house."

"I'm surprised he ever had sex again."

"Well, that's what I mean about going overboard. I only have one grandson now," she gestured to a wallet filled with photographs. "And I'm pretty sure it's because of that moment."

"That would do it for me."

"On the other hand," she winked. "He did have a condom, and we never had a teenage pregnancy."

"When can you start?"

"That's it?" Her body stilled.

"Well, I need to check your references, but yes. I'm sure." Someday, I hoped I'd be able to tell her, "You had me at the condom story." My life had been spent trading stories—telling my own, consuming those of other people. Here was a woman who stitched everything she was and wanted to be into her stories. There was no pretense, no warming up period. Just take me as I am, from day one.

"Next week?" she offered.

"Perfect."

We hugged goodbye. Martha moved methodically to her car. My own car smelled of stale donuts and dirty carpet. Thinking of Martha's description of her son's broken arm, I burst into tears. For perhaps the first time since Augie started working two hundred miles from home, I would not have to go it alone. This was what it meant to have backup, I realized, wiping tears from my cheeks.

Driving out of Jenkintown, I was happy. The idea of sharing the psychic responsibility of parenthood overwhelmed me. I didn't know what it was like to sit with another adult in a hospital waiting room, to depend on someone who was less than a three-hour drive away, even if it was for something as simple as watching the children while I escaped to the store to get a gallon of milk because we'd run out and they were screaming again for pygmy donkeys.

CHAPTER ELEVEN

BOTOX IN THE ELEVENTH HOUR

SEPTEMBER 2016
AMERICAN UNIFORM, NORTHEAST PHILADELPHIA, PA

On August 26th, I was back at Nineteenth and Fairmount. The employees were slightly less despondent than they had been in December. Like the rest of us, they understood that even though it was still ninety degrees, summer was slipping away. We needed to grab the days tightly, storing their colors and warmth for the winter ahead.

A nurse with fluffy sheep jumping across her uniform called me back and handed me the paper gown. A young woman was changing behind the waist-high privacy screen. We sat without talking, holding our clothes on our laps, while the office complex groaned awake, room by room.

"This is ridiculous." The young woman jiggled a foot. Her socks were ribbed and black, the kind you might borrow from your father for your first post-college interview. "Here, today, I mean."

"Yeah." I took my reading glasses off, more to admire them than to clean them. Kate Spade. New York. I'd gotten them the week before, after running over my old pair with the lawn mower. These were tortoiseshell with garden pink accents. "It took me five hours last time I was here. I'm Megan, by the way."

"Chloe," she said. "Nice glasses."

"Thanks. They're new." I twirled them by their striped temple ends. "I got them to look less like a mom."

Chloe looked blankly at me from behind impossibly hip cat-eye frames. "I don't even want to work for Philadelphia," she said. "My first choice is a suburban department, like Bristol. After this physical, I'm done with Philly." She cut her arm across her chest, an umpire declaring herself safe from the city. "I almost didn't pass the background test. They got hung up on the fact that I bought medical marijuana for a friend who had terminal cancer."

"Jesus." I leaned forward, my paper gown crinkling. "Where'd you do the fitness test?"

"At the academy. In the Northeast. It was horrible. Ninety-five degrees. People were puking." The memory of campus, of stunted row houses and barbed wire fences, rose between us. "The officers just stood on the side, and, like, watched us. Through clouds of cigarette smoke. Like they enjoyed it or something. It. Was. Fucked. Up." Her hand punched each word for emphasis. "Then they shouted at me for cheering people across the finish line. I was like, isn't this about 'the brotherhood' or something—"

"'Honor. Service. Integrity.'"

"Whatever. I'm worried they'll spin me today when they find out I'm taking prednisone. All I've ever wanted to be in life is a police officer." She rolled her ankle, testing young tendons and bones. "Sprained ankle. I'm two months out of the Criminal Justice program at the University of Scranton."

In the office across the hall, someone sprayed Lysol into the air, three short wheezes followed by an empty rattling sound.

"Williams." Nurse Janet opened the door. "You look familiar."

"I was here six months ago. Twice."

"Why are you back?" Janet asked, still holding the bottle of disinfectant.

"I really like it here."

Chloe snorted.

"Then you know the drill." Janet waved me into her office. "Touch your toes." The Lysol bottle landed in the trash can with a metal thunk. "Good, good. Rotate your arms. Backwards and then forwards. Nice. Now, balance and jump on one ankle. No problems with your health?"

"None."

"Then you're good to get drug tested." She scrawled her signature across my file, slapped it shut, and pointed me to the bathroom. I was shimmying into my pants when Chloe returned.

"I knew it." She crumpled her gown into a ball and threw it to the ground. "Spun for the steroids. They won't let me take the drug test—"

"But it's a prescription. You're taking them for an injury—"

"Doesn't matter." She grabbed her clothes. "Fucking police." The voice came from inside her sweatshirt.

I threw my gown next to hers. "Fucking police," I agreed. This phrase—not Honor. Service. Integrity—was the true chorus to the police recruit song.

"Williams." A new poster hung on the Chief Medical Officer's door: "The World Needs More Einsteins." She lifted her scissors. Logan Square. The Ben Franklin Bridge. No Auschwitz this time. Maybe I'd been mistaken. "Sit still." She grunted next to my ear. "You just need to get your urine receipt. Then you can leave." Her scissors clattered on the desk. I was discharged.

My drive home was aimless. I had nowhere to be and no official start date. Martha was watching the children. I took the long route, pulling off West River Drive to text Detective Brody. Boats dotted the river, water bugs skating across the surface. The August air blew across my open window, more like a subway train leaving the station than relief. A runner passed beneath the Strawberry

Mansion Bridge, squinting into the unrelenting light. We were exactly 3.1 miles from the Art Museum. This 8.4-mile River Loop was imprinted on my soul. All the quarter-mile hatch marks. All the conversations. Which water fountains to avoid, their mossy basins overflowing. My phone pinged.

> Megan,
>
> Hopefully the drug test will come back in time for you to make this class on September 5th. I can't say really how long it takes since it's done down at medical and I guess that depends on the amount of people. Keep your fingers crossed.

I rested my head against the steering wheel. In ten days, I might be starting a new job. Then again, I might not. I pulled the rear-view mirror close. The vinyl braid of the wheel had left a welt on my forehead, furrowing the skin. In the map of my face, wrinkles led to worry lines to laugh lines. Every line had been hard won, filled with pain and joy. Lately, when I looked in the mirror, my wrinkles spoke of a life half-over, to the children I could no longer have, to the books I would never write. I turned the car on. I might be old, and I might be lost, but I had an appointment to make.

On the drive to the suburbs, the air conditioning blew warm in my face, working overtime. At the top of Paper Mill Road, away from Philadelphia's gritty haze, the North Hills Country Club was opening its doors. A block over, a private school van idled, waiting for its campers to appear, faces blotchy from sleep and yesterday's sunburns. This was not the camp pickup of my childhood. The Ford Country Squire, equipped with wood-paneling, no air conditioning, a *School Bus* sign on the roof that had to be manually flipped upright, a third row of rear-facing seats, and a chain-smoking driver whose gray face we only ever knew in profile.

At the Rita's Ice stand on Willow Grove Avenue, I turned right. The parking lot of Skin Smart Dermatology was in the back, hidden from the street. From the outside, the office was opaque, with polarized windows and walnut accents. Inside, it had all the charm of an international departure lounge. Phil Collins sang in the background about an easy lover.

"I'd like to get Botox. Today."

The receptionist shook her head and traced the fuchsia script of her Samantha nameplate with a finger. "We're booking two weeks out. First available is September 9th."

"That works."

"First time?"

"Yes." The audio switched tracks. Phil was now reminding me about the memory of a face. If music were a paint color, Phil Collins would be beige putty. Apart from James Taylor, nothing was guaranteed to age me faster.

"Do you have something you want to look good for?" Behind reception, each cube in the wall of cabinets was backlit, containing exactly nothing.

"The police academy."

Samantha's body stilled for a moment. Then she started snapping to the synthesized brass opening of "Sussudio." "I just love this song." Her animal print blouse swished. "Botox takes two weeks to work. Do you still want the September appointment?"

"Yes." I retreated from the desk and Phil Collins. "I'll be back." Thirty-one years had passed since the release of *No Jacket Required*. I still had no idea what "Sussudio" meant or any desire to learn.

September 5th came and went without a phone call from the detective. An hour before my Skin Smart appointment on Friday, September 9th, an unknown number appeared on my phone.

"Megan, talk about leaving this until the last hour." As usual, Detective Brody began talking mid-conversation. I was pushing a full cart through Primex, the garden store. The hot-house air was stifling, smelling of cicadas that would never make it out of their seventeen-year gestation.

"Do you still want to do the academy?" Detective Brody's question was casual, a friend confirming a weekly coffee date. I stopped and pulled my T-shirt away from my neck, feeling the circle of wet.

"As in the police academy I was supposed to start last week?" The phone slipped through fingers greasy from bird suet. That morning Grace had been very specific with her Primex shopping list, telling me, "No more Red Fire Jalapeño suet, Mommy. The birds hate it."

"That very one." Detective Brody laughed. Fifty pounds of birdseed rested against my legs, threatening to topple me, to push me into a world where the only thing more absurd than my daughter's knowledge of the taste buds of woodpeckers was the fact that the police were calling on Friday with a Monday start date. "When can you come in to do the paperwork?" Detective Brody asked.

"I have appointments all day." I touched my forehead.

"Well, what time can you come in? It has to be today."

"Eleven? Will that give me enough time? School pick-up is at 3."

"Sure, sure." Detective Brody's request to start work—effective immediately, aside—this was the Philadelphia Police Department at its most flexible. "You just have to sign the paperwork with me, go downtown to get fingerprinted, and get your uniform. Plenty of time, plenty of time."

"I've already been fingerprinted." Chrysanthemums lined the parking lot, their sea-anemone heads heavy and tired, while landscapers hustled in and out of the greenhouse, carrying mulch and hardy asters.

"Headquarters needs you to do it again," the detective said. "Does 11 o'clock work?"

"That works."

"Great. See you soon. Bring your license and registration." Just like that, with a mundane list of everyday details—non-jalapeño suet, license, car registration, bird seed, a Botox appointment, and a vehicle title—I was on my way.

Skin Smart was a mile from Primex. My grubby hands pushed the heavy walnut door open. I wanted to make a joke about tilling old soil, but didn't. Phil Collins was still the soundtrack of choice, but now it was Genesis, not the mind-numbing soft rock of his later career. Clearly the Botox was working, transporting the office and the rest of us back to the seventies. The shots themselves—twelve, to be exact—hurt as much as one would expect from a needle filled with the world's most deadly natural toxin. That is to say, they stung only slightly less than the aesthetician's grimace when she asked me to wrinkle my face before the injections. Afterwards, she dabbed the pinpoints of blood on my forehead, handed me an ice-pack, and we were finished. My forehead ached, but I left Skin Smart somehow younger, full of hope.

My car registered ninety-two degrees on the drive to the re-cruiting center. The crystal-clear day stretched forever. It was another beach day, an unkept promise that summer would last forever. At the desk, I waited in line behind a man complaining about his mother's water bill. "You can't have a $3,000 water bill," the desk officer said. *Unless you're raising hippos,* I wanted to add. Five minutes passed. Now I was late; not for the first time, I wondered if I had the patience for this job, if I even wanted it anymore. The water-bill man retreated to a plastic chair and the officer buzzed me through.

"Congratulations!" Detective Brody clapped me on the back. His words rang hollow in the empty room. "Talk about getting in just under the wire."

"Yeah, thanks for that." The familiar hallway of vacant cubicles stretched away from us, each an anonymous carbon copy of its neighbor, each with a wheeled chair stalled on the lumpy carpet.

"Just a suggestion before we start," Detective Brody said. "Pick a designated driver this weekend. The PPD frowns on having to bail candidates out of jail for a DUI the weekend before the academy. You know, in case you celebrate getting into the academy too much."

A sub sandwich landed with a thump on the desk next to us. Bob was back from his lunch run. Deli meat and vinegar fought the smell of printer toner and won. After a two-year application process, Detective Brody and I were right where we'd started. Don't smoke a doobie. Remember to wear deodorant. Don't get a DUI.

"The academy is fun." Detective Brody winked. "Easy. Like high school. It's a life-changer." I thought of Westtown, of homesick orchard runs and the trunk room.

After copying my car title and registration, Detective Brody ushered me out the door for the last time. "Just ignore the officers at the academy," he said. "They like to yell a lot and try to intimidate you. They like to believe they're a paramilitary organization." Hands on his hips, he rocked his body forward, emphasizing the strength needed to graduate from the academy. "If you do what they tell you, you should be fine. Whatever you do, do *not* be late. And don't lie about being late. They know where all the traffic jams are." Maybe Detective Brody gave this advice to everyone. Maybe he saw something in me that needed correcting.

From the recruiting office, I drove to police headquarters for fingerprinting. The Roundhouse squatted in a patchwork of parking lots between Chinatown, Old City and the spaghetti-mess of ramps leading onto the Ben Franklin Bridge. I parked at 7th and Arch Streets. The Federal Detention Center loomed behind me, slitted windows staring down like so many blank eyes. Police headquarters was a honey-combed structure, a nest of interconnected circles. Every wall was curved. I circled upwards through a warren of old desks and chairs until I found the fingerprinting office. No men were working there. Pictures of children and pets lined the low cubicles. A radio played easy jazz.

"Over here." A woman with long acrylic pink nails waved. I sat with my wallet and hands in my lap. She moved papers and a clay coil pot aside.

"I have one of those." I pointed to the pot and smiled.

"Don't we all?" she said, including all the women in the office. "Don't we all." She patted the desk. "I'm gonna need both hands." My wallet slid to the floor. "You can put that on the table. Don't hide who you are."

"What?" I placed my wallet on the desk. It was hot pink and the size of a bread loaf.

"I love Kate Spade." She pressed my fingers into the ink pad. "Don't hide it. Flaunt it."

"Hot pink doesn't feel very police."

She tapped a pink nail against the leather, reminding me to remember her words. "Now you're going to need to hustle to get your uniform," she said, dismissing me.

For thirty years I'd lived in Philadelphia, yet I didn't recognize a single street name on the way from Headquarters to American Uniform, deep in the Northeast. People walked down roads that had no sidewalks and no trees. Big-box retail stores lay empty, reproached by miles of cement, a prison, and the derelict Tastykake factory.

Several patrol cars idled outside American Uniform. Inside the warehouse, the sheer volume of gear overwhelmed me. Body armor. High-visibility apparel. Handcuffs and self-defense equipment. Dress coats. All of it. I wanted to buy it all. Puffy rows of black tactical jackets surrounded the cash register. I passed my list to the saleslady. "I'll start a pile for you." She stepped around the men crowding the counter. "My name's Antoinette." I followed her frosted hair around the tall stacks of clothing, trying to avoid the officers.

"We have a problem." Antoinette dropped a huge pile of clothes in front of me. "We don't have pants smaller than a size 12."

"I'm sure that'll be fine." I grabbed the pile.

"What are you?" She stuck her head inside the dressing room. "A size 2?"

"Hardly." I stripped to my white cotton underwear and shrugged my legs into the baggy pants. "I'm a size 10. These are fine."

"You'll get in big trouble if you wear those pants." Antoinette pointed to where the fabric ballooned around my thighs and ankles. "They're too big. We'll both get in trouble." In the windowless store, her face was pale. Splotches of sunburn ran down her arms, remnants of a late-summer weekend down the shore. She stood, hands outstretched, waiting for me to return the pants. Two female officers stopped and took in the view. The clown-sized pants. The mismatched pink pom-pom socks. The pencil in my hair to keep my bun up. The Birkenstocks. I tucked a shirttail into my pants and straightened the blue and yellow *Police Officer* patch.

One of the officers was the red-haired alpha female who'd held my legs during the academy sit-up test. Everything about her sergeant's uniform was immaculate. She leaned against the metal rack then turned to her friend with a half-covered laugh. She and I had sat, nose-to-nose on a dirty gym mat, so close I could see the single eyebrow hair her tweezers had missed, could smell her fruity shampoo. At American Uniform, she had no memory of me. I was a joke. She and her partner had the badges. They were the popular girls. In the face of their mumbled comments, I was thirteen again, changing in the gym closet, hiding my flat chest.

The alpha officer walked to the front of the store, hand resting casually on her gun. "Give me a second," I told Antoinette, escaping behind the curtain. "Good idea about the pants." I threw them over the curtain rod. A mountain of gear sat on the dressing room stool. Long- and short-sleeved shirts. A tie. Belt. Socks. A pair of Rocky Alpha Force Zipper Waterproof Public Service Boots. *Proudly built for the men and women who serve and protect communities*, the oversized red and black box promised. Their logo was a bighorn sheep silhouetted against mountain peaks. Alpha Force was one word on the box—signaling a punch, a quick blow. With half-inch rubber treads, metal grommets, 1000-denier nylon fabric, and reinforced laces, these boots kicked down doors.

At the register, Antoinette separated the shirts from the rest of the pile. "Give me five minutes. I need to take the officer patches off your shirts." Shit. Shit. Shit. I stepped away from the register. Had I really been so stupid as to think that becoming a police officer was as easy as ironing on decals? This wasn't middle school. There was no reward, no participation trophy for simply passing the tests to get into the academy.

Two burly male officers entered the store, bringing the shimmering parking lot heat with them.

"Megan." The taller one stopped in front of the red-headed officer. "I saw you got promoted." He offered a hand in congratulation.

"I did." Silhouetted against the door, this Megan was petite and beautiful and a good ten years younger than I.

"Where are you now?" he asked. Both men were over six feet tall. Standing in front of Megan, they became a physical wall, excluding her partner.

"The academy." A fan cycled across the desk, blowing hot air and the acrid taste of disappointment over me.

"Like it?"

"Yes." She turned to browse through the stacks of children's clothing. The male officers slunk away.

Antoinette returned with my shirts. "When you graduate you can come back to get the patches." Folded neatly on top of my pile were two blue-collared shirts. Nothing more. "Take any of those you want," Antoinette told the two women, pointing to a pile of kids' shirts. "They're free." The women hurried around the stacked table, laughing as they ran into each other.

"How cute is this?" Megan held up a pink toddler shirt that said *I wear a bow, my mom wears a badge.*

"Sarah will love that," her partner agreed. "What about this for Jake?" Spread on top of the pile was a shirt that read, *Police Officer in Training.*

"I'm going to get these for my nieces and nephews, too," Megan said.

"How many can we take?" her partner asked. Neither woman looked like a mother. There were no smeared coffee stains on their pants, no signs of the subtle unraveling that signaled the upcoming end of the school day.

"As many as you want." Antoinette was busy tapping numbers into her register. "That's $350," she said, raising her head in time to catch me watching the women. I handed her my card. "You can take some, too." She waved toward the table. "Do you want a receipt?"

"No. I won't be returning anything."

Their arms full of T-shirts, the two female officers walked into the sunshine. Antoinette returned to folding pants behind the counter. I sidestepped to the kids' table and pushed two shirts into the bottom of my plastic bag. In ten months, when I graduated from the academy, I would have my patches and Gus and Grace would wear their shirts with pride.

CHAPTER TWELVE

SITUATIONAL AWARENESS

SEPTEMBER 12, 2016
POLICE TRAINING CENTER, NORTHEAST PHILADELPHIA

At 7:45 A.M., THE VACANT LOT that was 2900 Comly Road stared back at me. The collar on my new shirt itched. I was lost. The appointment letter had told me twice—in bold, caps, with three exclamation points—to report by *8 a.m. SHARP!!!* for the first day of the Philadelphia Police Academy. According to Google Maps, 2900 Comly Road didn't exist.

At 7:52, I U-turned across three lanes of rush-hour traffic to ask a parked cop for directions. "You're here for the academy," he said, eyeing my patchless blue uniform.

"Yes. My letter says to report to 2900 Comly Road."

"Huh?"

"Exactly."

"It's here." His words fell between the metronome clicks of his hazard lights. "Come on in." A long line of cars extended behind him. Doors slammed and people in brown uniforms bolted from their cars. Parking behind the last car, I ticked over the checklist in my mind. Lunch, pencil, *a folder that must be blue or black and not less than 2" wide.* Bag gaping open, I sprinted.

"Where're you going?" the gate sergeant asked.

"Auditorium."

"Wrong place." He motioned to an adjacent lot. "Park there. We decided to be nice to the recruits and let you park close on your first day." Maybe Detective Brody had given me the wrong address just to screw with me. Maybe I was too confident. Too old. Too academic. Whatever it was, he really showed me. I raced back to my car in the longest half mile of my life. Rocky Alpha Force Zippers—not so good for running. Polyester uniform—unbreathable, a glimpse of life before microfiber.

7:58 a.m. I was finally where I was supposed to be.

"Hurry, you're going to be late!" an officer directing cars yelled.

"I know, I know," I tossed back, continuing my mad dash.

"Well, at least she knows," another officer said.

7:59 a.m. Through the front doors, the same ones that had greeted me ten months earlier. I couldn't remember the last time I'd sat in an auditorium audience. Maybe ten years ago at the orientation for in vitro fertilization in San Francisco. The podium. That's where *I* was supposed to be. I sat on a plastic chair next to a kid with a blond crew cut and acne. He leaned into the guy next to him. "Army?"

"Yeah. You?"

"Yeah. Where?"

"Two years in Guatemala. Nothing major." His neighbors grunted their approval. If the blond one had enlisted at eighteen, right out of high school, he couldn't have been more than twenty. The department no longer required recruits to have two years of college coursework or the equivalent. In eight months, this recruit would be expected to respond to a domestic violence or rape call.

"Man, this one chick with blue eyes in Guatemala City—" Blondie began and then paused. The other guys dropped a shoulder, waiting to catch the end of his pause. "I should never have let her get away. She was something, uh huh, the moment I hit that—"

"Recruits, stand up and hustle!" A sparkplug of a man strode down the aisle screaming. A larger-than-life caricature, he was playing the drill sergeant in this movie. Eighty-nine recruits shuffled to the fire doors, bumping into one another like cattle. I passed the front desk. *Shock and Awe: Day One.* A sergeant caught me looking and flipped the folder over, its contents top-secret. Our bottle-necked group had maybe fifteen women. Out the door, through another, into the gym.

"Move! Move! What do you think this is? A walk in the park?" Five officers in dress uniform hurled commands at us. "Get in line, we don't have all day. Atten-*hut!*" Eighty-nine pairs of feet slid together. Eighty-nine backs straightened. Eighty-nine faces looked ahead, expressionless.

Ah, shit. I had no clue what those barked commands meant. A beat behind every order, I was transported back to the hell of middle-school gym. A boot appeared between my legs, almost knocking me down.

"Atten-hut means heels together, toes out, stand up straight, eyes forward, palms in, fists down the seams of your pants," an officer said. Little flecks of her saliva hit my neck.

Five sergeants glided silently between our rows, sharks on the hunt. "Fix your belt. You missed a loop." A finger jabbed my back. Balancing on my heels, I rethreaded my belt and ground my morning hope into the cement floor. Gone was the naive belief that the hazing rituals of my two-year application were a thing of the past, that the academy was about learning and serving our city.

"What are you?" Sergeant Sparkplug growled from the corner. "A moron? Does Mama need to help you get dressed in the morning?" *Is that you, John Wayne. Is this me?* Time collaged. I was in the gym, the smell of approaching fall mixing with the sweat of anxiety, but I was also an academic. Private Joker from *Full Metal Jacket* surfaced from my past. Two scenes unfolded simultaneously, one a movie, one real life.

Below the faded pennants of previous police academy classes, part of me retreated, watching the scene from above. In this gym, I was just like everyone else. Ordinary. A body. Nothing more. "DO NOT MAKE EYE CONTACT WITH YOUR SUPERIORS." Sergeant Sparkplug spoke only in bold caps. In profile, he was a good six inches shorter than I, face fleshy from shouting. He didn't walk. He strutted, one hand trigger-distance from his gun.

A female sergeant paused in front of me. She was older, her face twisted, either from pursing her lips in constant disapproval or from a rickety Eastern European childhood. "You need new barrettes. They must match your hair color."

Sadness punched through me. The night before, Grace and I had chosen my hair accessories. "Wear the polka dotted ones, Mommy," she'd demanded, neither of us imagining a world where the color of my barrettes mattered.

I'm not going to lie. I was scared shitless. Everything inside said *run like hell*. My inner third-grader pushed close—that little-kid part of me that always felt as if I'd done something wrong in the mercurial world of adults.

"You, you, you, and you." The sergeant pointed to four people. "Step forward. Give me twenty pushups for wearing long sleeves. Who the hell told you to wear long sleeves?" Four recruits assumed plank position. "Now count."

"One." The group sounded off.

"One, what?" Four sets of eyes widened.

"One, sir!" The sergeant answered himself with a shake of his head, baffled by their incompetence. "Now, do it again." On twenty, one of the women collapsed. "What are you doing, recruit? You aren't finished until you 'request permission to recover, sir.'"

"Request permission to recover, sir."

"Granted."

Sergeant Sparkplug stopped before a thin man wearing a gray suit. "What do you think you're wearing?"

The recruit tensed his shoulders. He had beautiful skin, the back of his neck smooth and brown. "A suit, sir."

"Why in the world are you wearing a suit?"

"Because they didn't tell me until Thursday that I was starting today. I worked all day Friday and Saturday." The recruit vomited his answer, words strewn together in a sickness. "The uniform stores are closed on Sundays. I didn't have time to get there after giving notice, I mean, before they closed." Peach fuzz dusted his upper lip. His shoes, polished to a high gloss, filled me with an unspeakable sadness.

"Work? You had work? What could possibly be more important than the police? Nothing. Nothing is more important than the police." The Sergeant jabbed a fist at us all. Honor. Service. Integrity. Sergeant Sparkplug was berating this young man for the exact qualities written across the PPD badges. He was punishing the recruit for the department's ineptitude, its complete and utter inability to use the U.S. Postal Service.

As Sergeant Sparkplug continued his tirade, the intertwined voices of my liberal arts education—Stanley Kubrick and Martin Luther King, Jr., to be specific—pulsed through my brain. *Injustice anywhere is a threat to justice everywhere.* Detective Brody had warned me about this. Sergeant Sparkplug was playing Ronald Lee Ermey, a copy of a copy. The officers were re-enacting Parris Island. But at what cost? What did it mean for the future, for our careers in law enforcement, that the police academy believed the making of a police officer began when eighty-nine recruits watched a blatant act of injustice and did nothing?

"There are some things you can't ever take back," I'd told Gus and Grace the day before. They'd been hurtling insults at me, fast and furious, because I wouldn't let them build a dirt bike course in the backyard.

"I hate you, Mommy!" Gus said. "I'm happy you're going back to work."

"Yeah," Grace tag-teamed her brother. "You're the meanest Mommy ever. A bad mother. You really suck at being a mom."

"That's one of the worst things you can say to me."

"So what?" Grace slammed the door. Close to tears, I'd thought about the nature of take-backs, about how we live life backwards and forwards, about how sometimes a thing is said or done that burrows deep inside your soul and never leaves.

The sergeants paced between us. I told myself this was only the first day. I'd had other rough starts. As a twenty-two-year-old PhD student at Temple University, I'd taught undergrads who grew up on the streets of North Philadelphia. "We used to tie a can to the tail of a stray dog and watch it run itself to death," one of them confessed to the class.

"Why?" I asked.

"Because that's what you do in North Philadelphia," another student answered.

"And it was fun."

"Recruit," Sergeant Sparkplug interrupted my memory. "Remember, nothing is more important than the police. Nothing."

"Yes, sir." The young man in the suit bowed his head.

"Drop and give me twenty."

Freshly-pressed jacket straining across his shoulders, pants dragging on the dusty floor, the young recruit reminded me of a puppy, gangly and not yet fully formed. Watching him pant, I was nauseated. I felt I'd just witnessed a group of adolescent boys run a dog to death, and I'd done nothing.

The gym door creaked open. A recruit scooted in, face sheepish. "Are you crazy?!" Sergeant Sparkplug exploded. "You're more than ten minutes late to the first day of the police academy."

"Sorry, sir, there was an accident."

"An accident? There are no accidents. An accident in the police department means you're dead. Tell that to your partner when he calls for backup. Drop and give me twenty." With two candidates on the floor, the sergeant swiveled his prehistoric blue eyes around the room. There was blood in the water here. He slid next to a young man with an almost comically wrinkled shirt.

"Recruit, where did you get that shirt?"

"Out of the package, sir." The recruit's voice was nasal in its immaturity. A fine sheen of adolescent depression coated his pudgy face.

"Out of the package." Sergeant Sparkplug barked his disgust. "Does that feel respectful to the shirt, recruit?"

"No, sir!"

The sergeant skated across the room, sensing another small vibration. "Recruits, stand still and look straight ahead. At nothing. You're looking at nothing. Now, you must iron a crease from the shoulder to the middle of the sleeve. Here." He drew an imaginary chalk line down the side of the cadet we weren't supposed to be looking at. "Every. Single. Night. You will iron your uniform." A homesick longing roiled through me. Augie had ironed my shirt and polished my shoes the night before.

"Drop and give me twenty. Ladies, while these recruits are working out, let me talk to you about hair color. If what is on your head is not your natural color, you will dye your hair back tonight. Tonight. If you have any piercings anywhere I cannot see, you will remove them. Tonight."

"Fix your belt." The female sergeant poked me from behind. "You've missed another loop."

A marching squadron entered the room. They wore last year's uniform, a cross between a postal worker's outfit and a parachute. "About face!" a voice drilled. Thirty people pivoted. The leader was a Hispanic woman. Pokerfaced, she moved next to the group, slightly off-center, a trailing tentacle to their giant jellyfish structure.

"The mission of the Philadelphia Police Department is to fight crime." Thirty people yelled this redundancy, voices rising and falling in waves. Clearly this was the *awe* part of today's program. "And the fear of crime, including terrorism, while safeguarding the constitutional rights of all people and working with our partners to provide service, enforce the laws fairly, apprehend offenders and prevent crime." With a final "forward march," they disappeared, a swell of voices leaving us to face the black hole that was Sergeant Sparkplug.

"For homework tonight, you will memorize the mission statement." Shit. I couldn't even put on a belt. "You will iron creases in your pants and shirt. You will trim each of your fingernails to an eighth of an inch. Don't think we won't inspect your hands tomorrow."

The polyester seams of my pants were scratchy beneath my fingertips. At American Uniform, I'd wanted the pants with the blue stripes.

"Those are lieutenant's stripes," Antoinette told me. "You have to earn those." At the academy, for maybe the first time in my life, my clothing revealed rank, not individuality.

"Step forward, recruit!" Sergeant Sparkplug ordered. A neat woman with perfectly oiled hair tiptoed to the center of the room. "Ladies, this is how your hair is supposed to look." Sergeant Sparkplug spun her around. As she twirled left, hesitated, then right, the gym morphed into the Wheel of Fortune, Sergeant Sparkplug was Pat Sajak, the female recruit Vanna White, existing only as a display model. Flip the letters, Vanna.

Today was Movie Day, and the winning phrase was "I—L-O-V-E—T-H-E—S-M-E-L-L—O-F—N-A-P-A-L-M—I-N—T-H-E—M-O-R-N-I-N-G." A self-satisfied flicker crossed the recruit's face. One hour into the police academy. This is who I'd become: For a brief moment, I wanted, more than anything, to be a mannequin with perfect hair.

"For every one of you standing here," Sergeant Sparkplug continued, "there are fifteen people who want to be, who didn't make it." Pride crept into the room, a slight lift in the men's shoulders. My shoulders didn't rise. I was too old, too tired, too cynical, to define success as a well-ironed shirt or perfect hair. These weren't difficult achievements. They weren't extraordinary. They were the Napoleonic rants of a middle-aged asshat. Not only was I standing next to Private Joker on the set of *Full Metal Jacket*, I was with Private Cowboy. *I think I'm going to hate this movie.*

"Atten-*hut*." The sergeant herded us back to the auditorium. "Move it! move it!" Ninety people treaded water with our feet, stomping the floor with new boots, pretending to move in the log-jam.

"Do you think this is a walk in the park?" a lieutenant jeered. He was skeletal, ashen—the only officer without a wedding band. If Sergeant Sparkplug scared me, Lieutenant Lurch was paralyzing. An arbitrary spitefulness clung to him, as if he only found peace in violent chaos. We shuffled back to our auditorium seats, slightly different people than we'd been when we'd left. Or maybe that was just me.

"Now we're going to go over some of the rules." Lieutenant Lurch took the stage while sergeants weaved through the aisles. A man and a woman adjusted a movie camera. "Fix your collar. Sit up straight." A huge officer nudged my shoulder. "More. And sit still. Keep your hands on your legs at all times."

"This isn't a job. It's a profession," Lieutenant Lurch began. "When we say be here at eight, we really mean seven. There are no excuses for childcare issues. If Little Jimmy has a cold," he scanned the room with a frown, emphasizing his complete dislike of children, "then you make a third, fourth, and fifth back-up plan. There are no snow days. If you can't drive in the snow, buy an SUV. If they don't plow your neighborhood, park on a street where they do and run to your car in the mornings. We fail people here. Don't think we don't."

"If you don't like the way the day has gone, you can leave." He offered us the door with a straight arm. "That's the exit. No harm. No foul. The police department isn't for everyone. And if you came here thinking you were going to try to change the department, don't. Just leave now. The police department doesn't need to change." On the sidelines, Sergeant Megan joined the older female officer. They stood, crisp white shirts almost touching, the space between them close, any objections as women to these rules long-ago erased by their rise through the ranks.

Rows of recruits stood rapt on either side of me. Eyes dead, they ate this up.

One of these things is not like the others. The *Sesame Street* anthem of my seventies childhood sang in my head. I wanted to step forward and raise my hand, to point to myself and say, "Mommy just doesn't belong."

"One last thing before we break for ten minutes," the lieutenant cautioned. "Recruits, when you see anyone who is a higher rank than you, you will yell 'make way' and hug the wall. This trains you to become situationally aware of your environment. As a police officer, you need to know what's going on around you at all times. We need to teach you this." The recruits nodded their unified agreement.

"Step onto the platform." The lieutenant pulled a young man from the first row. "You are now going to demonstrate how to 'make way.'" As the lieutenant positioned the recruit, part of me retreated. Recruits had to learn how to navigate Philadelphia as police officers, but I wasn't sure how stepping aside in a hallway got us there. Surely everyone here saw "make way" for what it was: a rationalization of an archaic command structure. As a mother, I carried a unique situational awareness that could never be forgotten. Stairs. Glass tables. What began as an ankle-high world quickly expanded once Gus and Grace learned to crawl. When they pulled themselves upright, the high-water danger-line of our lives rose, flooding a room with objects now within grabbing distance. A bottle of Benadryl left open on a sink meant a late-night call to poison control. Scissors discarded on a chair ended in six stitches in the emergency room. If the police department wanted recruits to be aware of their environment, all they had to do was hire more mothers. Or send them to IKEA with two toddlers.

On the stage, the recruit remained locked in a formal box step with his lieutenant, while I slid backwards, into the past.

Gus and Grace were three, and we were shopping for big kid beds. "One hand on the cart at all times," I warned over our stack of boxes and mattresses. In the checkout aisle, the front wheel turned sideways, jammed by a blue and yellow tag. My sheet sets spilled to the floor.

"Let me help." The college student behind me stepped forward. She was holding exactly one frying pan.

"Leave them." I waved the cotton trains and rainbows aside. "They never fit the mattresses anyway." In the warehouse behind us, a joyful shrieking began, threading its way through the aisles.

"Jesus Christ," the college student said. "Whose kids are those?"

"Is one of them naked?"

"Yes."

"Chasing the other with a giant feather duster?"

"Yes."

"Those would be mine." The smell of Swedish meatballs hung everywhere, coating me with a familiar claustrophobia.

"Well," she slapped the frying pan against her knees as the line moved forward. "At least they found you."

"Oh, they were never lost." What I didn't tell her was that I always knew where my children were in IKEA. I also knew the location of every emergency exit. *Utgång*. In case I decided to make a run for it. Alone. This was the unique situational awareness every mother possessed.

"Hustle on your breaks." Lieutenant Lurch's directions pulled me away from IKEA. "*Everyone* here is of a higher rank than you. It might take you fifteen minutes just to get out the front door."

Outside, the sun surprised me. Two women huddled, backs set against the building like emperor penguins. "Holy shit," the smaller one said, dipping her chin to her chest. "It's so cold in there." It was 10:15 a.m. Fall warmth spread across our shoulders and foreheads, while inside, the air conditioning continued to blow full blast.

"Hey." The smaller woman motioned for me to join. "I remember you. You were at my academy test." She turned to the other woman. "No, I mean this chick really ran. I was huffing and puffing, and she was *out*." She flung a hand into the distance, as if I'd been swallowed by the Great Northeast. "There were guys there, hunched over after she blew by them, going like, 'What the hell just happened to me?'"

"Did you run that day?" I asked.

"Yeah." One hand touched her hair, parted X-Acto-knife straight. "Then I went straight to the emergency room and got my tonsils out. I had an infection. Passed out. Luckily, they let me take it again."

"Megan."

"Janai."

"Lupe." The second woman nodded at me. She was compact, a solid coil held together by an economy of motion.

"Did you see that squad leader? The one shouting the commands? That's who I want to be," Janai said without waiting for us to answer. "How do you think you get to do that?"

"No idea." The possibility hadn't even occurred to me. Cross-country team captain, sure. Class valedictorian, yes. Phi Beta Kappa, fuck yeah. Squad leader? Never.

"I'm more worried about getting here on time every morning," Lupe admitted.

"I was here at 6:15 a.m.," Janai said.

"Wait, what?" Nothing about Janai's ironed pants suggested she'd spent the morning sleeping in her car. "What the hell did you do for an hour and forty-five minutes?"

"I waited. Maybe dozed off a little. I was just so scared of being late."

The cold of the auditorium remained, rooted deep within my body, and I shivered, a world of difference opening between me and my academy class. This wasn't the peer group of the fitness test. Janai and Lupe were twenty years younger than I.

An aluminum taco truck rattled into the driveway and parked, covering us with Shakira and greasy exhaust.

"I'm going to get here at six every morning," Janai said, ignoring the truck. "My husband's police, too. He's just coming home when I'm heading out."

"Do you guys have kids?" Lupe asked.

"Yep." Janai held up three fingers as proof. "Five, three, and one-and-a-half. I had to beg. Beg, I tell you, to get the sitter to pick them up at 6:15 a.m."

A scrawny teenager in an apron hustled to raise the concession window on the truck.

"I'm a single mom during the week. My husband works north of Scranton," I said, turning as the sun glinted off the aluminum door.

"Jesus, that smells good." Lupe pointed to the truck.

"Yeah," Janai agreed. "I'm starving."

"I'm a single mom," Lupe said. "My baby's daddy just got home from being deployed. He takes her during the week so I can sleep and focus on my career. I get my baby back on the weekends."

The three of us stood apart from the rest of the crew-cuts milling about aimlessly. "How old's your baby?" I asked Lupe.

"Two." When she smiled, Lupe was beautiful, her face full of an earthen wisdom.

"Not seeing your daughter during the week must be so hard." Lupe shrugged my pity away. "It's to give her a better life."

"How many kids do you have?" Janai asked me.

"Two eight-year-old boy-girl twins."

"Nice job," she and Lupe chorused. "Jinx." They laughed and slapped hands. To them, twins were a sign of personal strength, not laboratory luck and a journey filled with bedpan bedrest and pygmy donkeys.

"Yeah," I pumped a fist. "One and done."

"I hope we're all in the same squad," Janai said. Behind us, the building doors opened and closed on shouts to "make way."

"That would be awesome," Lupe agreed. I said nothing. Lupe pointed to the door. "We should go back now." My feet, leaden in their Alpha Force Zippers, carried me and an ever-expanding emptiness back to the auditorium.

CHAPTER THIRTEEN

A THOUSAND PAPER CUTS

SEPTEMBER 12, 2016
POLICE TRAINING CENTER, NORTHEAST PHILADELPHIA

"ATTEN-*HUT!*" SERGEANT SPARKPLUG STRODE TO THE PODIUM. "Take a seat and pass your driver's licenses to the end." License after license landed on my lap. They made a pile not unlike the Topps baseball cards we used to buy at Frank's penny candy store on Commonwealth Avenue, the gum brittle and stale. I dealt mine to the bottom. It was one of a few cards printed horizontally, the sign of being twenty-one or older in Pennsylvania.

"Let's see what this class is about." The sergeant shuffled his papers. "Stand up if you're former military." Lupe and half the class stood.

"Who's under thirty?" More students rose.

"Over thirty?" Ten candidates got to their feet.

"Over forty?" I stood alone.

"Enough of that." Sergeant Sparkplug waved an arm, marking forty the end of the line at the police academy. "Stand if you have an associate's degree." The angry rash that had covered his cheeks earlier had receded, turned pasty white by the relentless forward march of bureaucracy. Maybe thirty chairs pushed back.

"College?" Twenty people remained standing. In the row in front of me, a recruit whispered. "I was supposed to start Temple this fall."

"Hey, me, too." His neighbor high-fived him. "Fifty thousand dollars from the police seemed a lot better than school," the second said, his crewcut new and indistinguishable from his neighbor's. Both were putting-green soft, ending in the neat white line of a summer spent outdoors.

"Anyone have a master's degree?" The questions continued while the HVAC system filled the auditorium with a low static hum. I stood, alone again, sweat ponding between my shoulder blades. *One of these things is not like the other.* "Enough of that." Sergeant Sparkplug turned the page, relegating higher education to life's blank underside. "Have a seat. When I read the name on your license, stand up and announce your sex and race. Elizabeth Blackwell?"

A slight woman on the other side of the auditorium rose. "Male, white," she said. "Um." She covered her face with her hands. "I mean, female, white."

"You sure about that, recruit?"

"Yes, sir!"

"Up here, I don't care *what* you are." He spread his fingers, welcoming us into the open-minded kingdom that was the Philadelphia Police Department. "They just need to write this down in the back. Can you repeat it?"

"Elizabeth Blackwell, female, white."

He shook his head and broke down laughing. "Take ten everyone."

Outside the auditorium, twenty men waited in line for the bathroom. The cloying smell of pink hand sanitizer filled the women's room. A recruit was fixing her hair in the mirror.

"First time it pays to be a woman, right?" I said. An automatic faucet turned on, splashing us. She blotted the front of her shirt and said nothing. Maybe I wasn't funny, or maybe we were all Elizabeth Blackwell inside. Bathroom lines aside, no one needed to tell us that it was always better to be "male, white" at the academy.

A woman with a pixie haircut unbuttoned her shirt and punched the hand dryer. "It's so fucking cold in there." She rubbed her arms beneath the hot air, rotating the metal nozzle so it blew down her front, pillowing the blue fabric and exposing the crenellated top of a black lace bra. "Holy cow that feels good." She gave a little wiggle, and I laughed. "What do you guys think of the first day so far?" she asked. One of the dryers cycled off.

"Pretty much what I thought," a woman behind me said.

"About what I expected," another added. There were maybe five women in the bathroom. Most of the stalls were empty. The toilets flushed automatically, whooshing on and off, punctuating the unique conspiracy of silence that was the academy.

Back in the auditorium, Lieutenant Lurch reappeared. He and the sergeant were taking turns speaking, a version of good-cop, bad-cop without the good. "Before we hear from the Fraternal Order of Police," he said, "I want to go over a few academy rules. From my experience, people get thrown out for two reasons: their mouth and their behavior. Do what you're told, and don't go out and get drunk or try to break up a bar fight. There's no smoking here at the academy." He stopped and surveyed the room. "How many of you smoke?"

For once, no one volunteered.

"Very good." He winked. "If you did smoke, you made the wise choice to quit before the academy." Stained fingers turned the page of the orientation booklet. Lieutenant Lurch had been one of the officers chain-smoking on the sidelines of my fitness test. "Now, let's talk fitness." I sat up. Maybe this was the part of the program where we ran a timed mile in our uniforms, where I finally got to be a part of something.

"To enter the academy," the lieutenant said, "you need to be in the top seventy percent of people off the street. To graduate, you need to be in the top fifty. This is a crime. This is disgusting." He scratched the papery yellow skin on his neck. "But it's what the state tells us." I deflated. There would be no running today. When we graduated, half of the criminals we chased would be able to escape. No wonder cops resorted to guns.

"Now, ladies," Lieutenant Lurch searched for us in the audience. "This is important. If you become pregnant, you need to tell us. Immediately. The safety of your unborn child depends on it." My legs crossed in protest. There were "no excuses for childcare issues" at the academy, but the PPD certainly had a lot to say about my unborn children. A hand tapped my shoulder, pointing for me to put both feet on the floor.

This is the way the world ends, I thought, shifting my weight. *Not with a bang but a whimper.*

"On that note," the lieutenant said, "I'd like to introduce the President of the Fraternal Order of Police."

John McNesby grasped the podium with swollen fingers. "We're cops helping cops," he said. "We have a lot of money at our disposal, close to a trillion dollars." Surely I'd misheard. A trillion dollars would put the FOP in the top twenty of developing nations, based on gross national product. "Take these, take these." He handed a stack of business cards to the front row, jowls hanging mastiff-like over his collar. "Anytime you have a problem, call me. You get in a bar fight. Call me. I had a woman three weeks into the academy. She wanted to quit. We persuaded her not to. Now she's a great cop. We like questions in the police department." He patted sweat off his forehead with a handkerchief. "Call us with your questions. Anytime. Now, let's get to the paperwork. Your date of hire is today: September 12, 2016. The most important day of your life."

Eighty-nine hands wrote down the date. I hesitated. Forced to pick the most important day of my life, I was going to have to go with May 14, 2008, the day Gus and Grace were born. Or maybe the day Augie and I were married, although I could never remember when that was. November 20, 1969, my birthday, was a close contender.

"September 12, 2016," McNesby repeated. A sacred-like quiet descended on the room. "You will never forget it." The recruits bowed their heads, members of the newly converted. "Now we need to talk about something important," McNesby continued, after a respectful pause. "Death benefits. We all know bad things happen to cops. The FOP contracts with the City of Philadelphia to give you a $25,000 insurance policy, on and off duty. Accidental death, or killed in the line of duty, doubles the face value—$25,000 becomes $50,000. If you remain a member in good standing, the FOP carries a $5,000 policy on you. [5] On page two, you need to list beneficiaries, the people who will get this money when you die—"

"My mom's gonna be pretty excited about this," one of the crewcuts announced, resting his pencil on the blue and white form. "She's gonna be rich when I die."

His neighbor gave him a thumbs up, scribbled "Mom" across his form, leaving second and third beneficiaries blank. Never in my job history had an employer been so fixated on my potential death or placed so little monetary value on my life. At the minimum, my family would receive $30,000 if I died. If I maxed out all these benefits and died from any cause except suicide before I retired, my family would get $120,000. My credit-card death benefits paid out better than the PPD.

"One last thing." McNesby snapped the orientation booklet closed on the inevitability of our deaths. "The FOP has its own computer system which is not attached to the city. Keep your beneficiaries up-to-date. Fellas," he pointed to the male congregants. "I guarantee that the girlfriend you have today will not be the girlfriend

---

[5]   In addition, the FOP offered two extra policies. The first was for $7,500. Accidental death or killed in the line of duty doubled the face value. The policy had to be in place so that you could purchase a second policy of greater value, if you wanted. You could purchase $10,000, $25,000, or $50,000.

or wife you have in fifteen years. In fifteen years, you won't even remember her name." Cheers and hoots rippled through the rows, toppling recruits like dominoes.

"I'm gonna stick with Mom," the crewcut said.

Gunnery Sergeant Hartman and the set of *Full Metal Jacket* had returned. *Your days of fingerbanging ol' Mary Jane Rottencrotch through her pretty pink panties are over!*

"These benefits are a great value. All we ask in return," McNesby broke midsentence for effect. Here came the smarmy part. The hard sell. The Pontiac Firebird I'd been waiting for since I first saw him fingering his rhinestone tie-clip. "All we ask to make this available to you is your five-dollar dues." Eighty-nine recruits opened their wallets. Not me. Our packing checklist had said to leave cell phones and wallets in our cars. "If you don't have money, get an envelope and mail it in."

"No!" Lieutenant Lurch stepped forward with a roar. "No one leaves this room without paying. I'm not tracking you down for your union dues. I don't care if you have to scrounge pennies from the back seat or borrow from the guy behind you. No one leaves without paying."

"Hey," I turned to the guy on my left. "My wallet's in my car. Can you spot me five dollars?" Half-way through day one at the police academy, I was begging a stranger for money in a union shakedown.

"Sure." He peeled a bill out of his wallet and dropped it in my lap, careful not to touch me. All the talk about transitory girlfriends and pregnancy had made being female at the academy a contagion best avoided.

"What's your name?" I asked. "I'll pay you back tomorrow."

"Lopez." We both knew he wouldn't remember what I looked like tomorrow.

"Thanks." I walked to the back of the auditorium where Lieutenant Lurch took my money and union paperwork, his open palm erasing the line between legal and criminal coercion.

Once the money was collected, McNesby gave the podium to a woman. She carried a gun and wore black high heels that gaped midsole when she walked. "In your packet, you will find the form to donate pre-tax to the FOP Political Action Committee. You don't have to do it, but most people do." Eighty-nine pencils checked the donation box. I couldn't stop myself. My hand rose, pulled by a puppeteer or the ghost of my liberal self. "Yes?" She pointed a frosted nail at me.

"What presidential candidate does this PAC endorse?"

"Oh." She adjusted a ponytail streaked the ashen-colorless blond of diners and New Jersey roundabouts everywhere. "I don't think they do that." McNesby nodded for her to continue. "We don't endorse presidential candidates." This time she said it with confidence. "Lodge Number Five is here to represent your interests." A man walked up to the stage to reposition the camera. Something was about to happen. Bodies rustled around me, impatient with my question. I checked the box. I was now financing "Make America Great Again."[6]

"Atten-*hut*. The Police commissioner of Philadelphia, Richard Ross." Officers snapped to attention, backs against the wall, heels together in full salute. Silence descended on the room as a personable and attractive man strode to the front, shaking hands down the line.

"Now, I want to talk about what's been going on in the media." He rolled up his sleeves and tipped forward, as if this were an intimate conversation between us and him. As he spoke, the AC cycled on again, trying to fill the room, to replace air that had turned sacred and thin. "In my humble opinion," Ross said, "there isn't a problem

---

[6] That evening, the news announced that the FOP would endorse Donald Trump for president, and McNesby told CBS the Philadelphia Chapter would follow. See Claire Sasko: "Reactions Mixed After Philly's FOP Endorses Trump." *Philadelphia Magazine.* 19 September 2016. (https://www.phillymag.com/news/2016/09/19/philly-police-fop-trump/).

with the police. The police are good. Yes, there are bad police." He stroked his mustache with his thumb, a lampshade so closely shorn it was more shadow, more second upper lip, than mustache.

"What we see now is the result of a certain number of people wanting to get in front of the media," he continued. "It's all a media frenzy." The auditorium nodded in agreement. "That's the most important thing I can leave you with." A group of officers encircled him, forming a protective cell wall around him. In an instant, a flurry of formality, he was gone, sucking the power out of the room.[7]

"Dismissed for lunch," Lieutenant Lurch announced.

I made my way to Janai and Lupe. "You guys going outside?"

"No," Janai said. "I'm going to stay here so I won't be late."

"I have paperwork to do," Lupe said.

Outdoors, recruits stalled, silent and shell-shocked. The checklist hadn't included lunch. Those who had money bought tacos from the truck or ate vending machine snacks. A few candidates sat on benches, balancing Tupperware on their laps.

"Jeez," I pointed to a male candidate's chicken and rice. "Can I have some?"

"I know, right?" He stopped mid-spoonful, long enough to let me know we wouldn't be friends. "My girlfriend made it for me last night."

Twenty minutes later, the lunch truck window banged shut and the engine sputtered alive. We filtered back through the doors of the academy, trading sharp September sun for fluorescence. Traffic slowed around a table where a group of female officers was chatting, ignoring us. Pieces of conversation drifted outward.

---

[7] Ross served as Police Commissioner of Philadelphia from January 2016 to August 20, 2019. He resigned in 2019 when two former police officers filed a sexual harassment and retaliation suit against him. Three years after Ross's resignation, a jury ordered Philadelphia to pay $1 million dollars to the plaintiffs. (https://www.inquirer.com/news/philadelphia/philadelphia-police-lawsuit-richard-ross-sexual-harassment-retaliation-20220524.html).

"I really want to run Broad Street for the first time this year," Sergeant Megan said, throwing an arm across the back of her neighbor's chair. "I've been running a lot."

I almost said that I'd run Broad Street more than ten times. That my best pace was 6:40. That I would be happy to help train with her. That I'd once been crazy enough to run from the finish to the start as a warmup.

"Keep moving." Hands pushed me from behind. "We're going to be late."

I tripped, embracing the wide blue back in front of me as the group pulled me upright and swept me forward. The women's conversation faded into the background, as did all the things I wanted to say.

Inside, the auditorium smelled of Cheetos and stress sweat. We sat, and the interminable parade of benefit representatives continued. Matronly women from the pension plan arrived, looking like bank tellers in their polyester pantsuits.

"We offer two plans," they said, handing out one form. "The one you should choose is Police Plan B. The other one is offered by the city, and it's crap." There were no prospectuses, no financial forecasts. Once again, I signed. By now, we'd been sitting in the auditorium for close to six hours listening to our benefits. Except they weren't really our benefits. They were talking points, choices other people had made for us.

"Atten-*hut*." Lieutenant Lurch returned with another pamphlet, this one with the mission statement on the front.

"Read," he ordered.

Class #381 recited the lines after him.

"Again."

We read with all the passion of a middle-school strings concert.

"And again." The paragraph was less than fifty words, but it was an empty space, a blankness that swallowed me. Each candidate brought a different rhythm to the words, making an overlapping chorus.

"Stop, Stop!" The lieutenant waved his arms at us, a conductor canceling our performance. "What are commas for?" he asked.

This I knew. My fingers tapped through the rules. 1.) After an introductory element or clause; 2.) to separate independent clauses; 3.) around appositives that do not contain essential information—

"Commas are for pauses," the lieutenant said, giving eighty-nine people the wrong answer. "So pause." We tried again, our words and sentences still colliding. The lieutenant shook his head. "Now turn the paper over under your seat and read." The group began, but I couldn't remember a single word. Not a single word. I lip synched as if I were in church, flipped my sheet over, and started cheating.

"Work on this tonight and remain standing. Raise your hand and repeat the Oath of Office after me."

In an anonymous room in Northeast Philadelphia, I solemnly swore to "support, obey, and defend the Constitution of the United States." I would like to say that the oath made me shiver, that it felt momentous. Certainly there were recruits who teared up that day with pride and emotion. I was not one of them. During the six hours of presentations, a fissure had opened deep within me. I simply did not believe the oath, did not believe that the Philadelphia Police Department operated "without consideration to a person's race, color, sex, gender identity, religious creed, sexual orientation, age, national origin, or ancestry."

In a blur of meaningless details, officers taught us how to compute our height in inches and how to sign our names to a list of *Background Information Amendments*. We were told things we already knew: we had to be Philadelphia residents, we had to leave our exercise gear in the gym and our phones in our cars. They explained what a doctor's note needed to include, how the department reimbursed expenses. This was death by a thousand paper cuts. Each a single sliver of pain, barely noticeable, but when counted in aggregate, the pointlessness of it all hurt.

"Before we take ten," Lieutenant Lurch instructed, "just sign the final page of the packet and leave it on your seats."

PHILADELPHIA POLICE DEPARTMENT TRAINING BUREAU
CERTIFICATE OF AGREEMENT

In consideration of receiving certified Municipal Police Officer Training along with compensation and medical benefits during training, the undersigned hereby agrees to reimburse the City of Philadelphia in full, all payments made to or on behalf of the undersigned in the event he/she fails to remain in active employment by the Philadelphia Police Department for a continuous period of two years immediately following the initial certification of the undersigned by the Pennsylvania Municipal Police Officer's Education and Training Commission (MPOETC).

However, this agreement shall not apply in the event the undersigned is unable to complete a continuous period of two years due to (a) death of the undersigned, (b) if the undersigned is laid off from employment, (c) any active or reserve military duty commitments of the undersigned, or (d) if the undersigned becomes physically unable to perform the duties of a Police Officer.

Date:_____

_____

(Police Recruit Officer)

The world around me stilled. A fluorescent ceiling panel faltered then brightened before shorting out with a pop. I threw the packet on my chair and left the auditorium.

The sky stretched away from the academy, an oppressive blue, more tent canopy than possibility. "Did you see that contract they want us to sign?" I asked Janai and Lupe.

"Which one?" Janai said. The day had taken its toll on her, pulling gently at the skin beneath her eyes.

"The one that says we have to pay the city $49,000 if we quit or don't give them two years after graduation."

"No, no, no." Janai shook her head. "My husband says it costs them $4,500 to send each of us through the academy. If we leave, that's all we'd owe them back."

"I hope so, because I can't sign that," I said.

"No, no, you misread it."

"I'm going back in."

Several recruits slumped in auditorium chairs they hadn't left all day, their bodies placeholders in the mountain of details the PPD had built around us. Lieutenant Lurch leaned against the wall, long limbs folded in on themselves like a half-dead spider.

"Excuse me, sir. Can I ask you a question?" He opened his eyes, and I turned to the last page of the booklet. "Can you tell me what the *compensation* mentioned here means?" I pointed. "Is it the $4,500 tuition you spend to put us through the academy or the $49,000 in salary the city pays us?"

"It's your salary and benefits," he said, covering me with the taste of a week's worth of cigarettes.

"Oh, okay." I backed away, returning to my seat. "Thank you." My section of the auditorium was now dim, the dead fluorescent panel a rotten tooth in the ceiling grid. Goose pimples ran up the back of my neck and down my arms. I couldn't stop shaking. Two years I'd spent applying to the department and no one had mentioned this. Even worse, they'd put it on the last page, telling us to sign without an explanation, as an aside, at the end of a long day. This was death by a thousand paper cuts where the last was a knife to the gut.

I didn't understand. The PPD wasn't the US Army. It wasn't Temple University twenty-five years ago. Then, I'd been a twenty-two-year-old teaching assistant walking into an auditorium much like this one. Day one of my graduate career. Time to sign up for my health benefits, which Temple paid, along with my tuition and a salary. Not once during those nine years did Temple tell me that if

I didn't finish my PhD program, I'd have to repay my entire tuition, salary, and benefits. I couldn't sign this. I couldn't hold my family hostage for two years. The doors behind me banged open and the heavy footfalls of returning recruits filled the room.

"Stand up when I say your name." Sergeant Sparkplug was in the center aisle, dealing our licenses back. Someone, probably one of the bank tellers, had organized the stack in reverse alphabetical order. "Williams," he began.

I sat, waiting for a first name.

"Williams," he said, louder this time, searching for an empty chair that meant someone had made a run for it.

"Here, sir." I stood and held out my hand.

"What were you waiting for?" The sergeant stepped toward me. "A handwritten invitation?"

"No, sir!" Each of my words parsed a single piece of anger. "I was waiting for you to call our first names in case there was more than one Williams."

"Learn your name, recruit." The sergeant pivoted, dismissing me with a turn of his heel.

Licenses returned, Lieutenant Lurch glided back to center stage. "Before we move forward, we need to talk about how you address your superiors in the police department. On our last break, someone asked me a question about the agreement you just signed."

He hunted for me in the audience. "You need to learn how to ask a question of a superior officer. Rank, then last name. You need to abandon your civilian ways. You are no longer civilians." He drew an arc with his tobacco-stained index finger to include us all. "Police work is different from any other job. It's 90 percent sheer boredom and 10 percent utter terror."

My hands curled into fists. This room was a dangerous place, governed by rules I would never understand. Here, I could be humiliated in front of a hundred people for asking a respectful question about my financial future. According to the lieutenant, you abandoned your former personhood the moment you took the Oath of Office. I knew some basic Latin: "Civ. As in *civitas* or the body of citizens who constitute a state." In my world, police were citizens *and* public servants. It wasn't an either/or proposition. After all, a few short hours before, the President of the FOP had reassured us of the department's innate humanism when he said, "the police like questions."

"Follow the sergeant. You're going on a walk." The lieutenant pointed to an emergency exit door. We scattered, bats in the sudden daylight. A round sergeant led us through the chain-link fence that surrounded the academy. Field thistle grew along the fence line, its spiked heads and armored leaves crowding what should have been grass.

"As the youngest class on campus," Sergeant Cherub explained, a slight wheeze connecting his words, "you'll park on Comly Road each morning. It's half a mile from the academy. There aren't enough lockers inside, so you can't store anything here. Bring your bags with you every morning."

The very ordinariness of the day outside the academy surprised me. On the four-lane road next to us, parents drove to pick up their children, to the grocery store, distracted by the errands that defined daily life and the endless red lights of Northeast Philadelphia.

"Today we made an exception for you and let you park next to the building," the sergeant said. "Do not park in front of the barricades tomorrow. Now I want you all to walk to the parking spots yourself to show me you understand." Ninety people converged on the cement, colliding like bumper cars before stuttering to a stop. We stood, motionless and sapped of electricity. "Now let's go back," the sergeant pointed. It had taken us an hour to preview our parking spots—the perfect ending to a day that could have been condensed into a one-page memo.

Janai, Lupe, and I retraced our path, stepping over asphalt seams turned gooey in the heat. "A fifteen-million-dollar new facility." I said, welcoming the building's coolness. "And they can't give us parking or lockers—"

"I'm gonna have to get here at 5:45 a.m. now," Janai interrupted.

"Yeah. What the hell is that about?" I asked. "L.A. Fitness has better benefits."

Janai and Lupe didn't laugh. Our group squeezed through the emergency exit. "I asked the lieutenant about that 'compensation' thing I was talking about," I said.

"Oh, yeah?" Lupe stepped away from me

"If we quit, we have to pay back $49,000. Not just the $4,500 tuition."

"Oh well," Janai shrugged. "I guess they own my ass for the next three years."

"I can't quit," Lupe said. "I have a job once I graduate. In Bristol—"

"No foot patrol in Bristol," Janai added with a laugh. "You ain't stupid."

"Hells yeah." Lupe high-fived us, bringing our group back together. "They hired me because I speak Spanish, and I'm a vet. It's for a better life for my daughter, you know."

Janai and I both nodded. I knew what she meant. Then again, I didn't. I had options beyond the Philadelphia Police Department. Teaching. Coaching. Writing. Augie made a decent salary. We owned our house. We had some savings. I wasn't trapped, at least not financially. The police did not own my ass.

Class #381 stood in the auditorium where the day had begun. A list of victims scrolled through my head: Trayvon Martin, Ernest Satterwhite, Dontre Hamilton, Eric Garner, Darren Wilson. More people and names than I could remember. Eight hours at the academy had bored me to death and broken my heart. The minute our polished boots hit campus, we became members of a shoot-first-ask-questions-later culture.

From Sergeant Sparkplug, I'd learned how to be bullied and, more importantly, how to stay silent when someone else was bullied. I'd learned not to ask questions. From being forced to join the union, pressured into giving money to a PAC, to disclosing my race, sex, age, and education in public, I'd learned that the police operate in some very gray legal areas, if not fully outside the law. No wonder Black men in our communities were being shot dead.

Standing before our plastic chairs, Class #381 deflated. It was 4 o'clock. If they'd dismissed us an hour ago, instead of walking us down Comly Road, Gus and Grace could have avoided after care. But nothing was more important than the police.

"Atten-*hut*." Sergeant Sparkplug welcomed us back. "Class dismissed."

With a rustle of papers, we dispersed. A few of the military guys stalled in the parking lot, congregating next to pickups and jeeps. Inside my hot car, my polyester uniform clung to me like Saran Wrap. I ducked my head, hiding. The tears came fast and furious. Moisture condensed on the windshield, turning the car into my own personal terrarium. Nails, creases, mission statement, *civitas*. Tears dripped onto my phone. I typed *civilian*.

1. *Noun.* A person not in the armed services or the police force. Synonyms: noncombatant, nonmilitary person, ordinary civilian, private citizen. *Informal: civvy.*

I laughed wetly. Go figure.

Lieutenant Lurch was right. Becoming a police officer was a Faustian bargain, a deal with the devil. I would no longer be "ordinary"—a stay-at-home mom or a failed writer. But to protect civilians in the United States, to even be a police recruit, you had to carry an insurmountable loss—the untethering of your basic humanity.

CHAPTER FOURTEEN

JUST ME

Traffic on the far side of campus stuttered, gridlocked in an asphalt haze. Windows sealed, my car inched away from the academy. I punched numbers into my phone.

"Hello?" Augie asked. By now I was crying so hard I couldn't speak.

"Hello? Megan? Are you okay?"

"Yeah." A round of dry heaves punched me in the gut.

"Do you have that stomach thing again?"

"No." I turned right onto Comly Road and laughed. "I hate the PPD. I won't sign the contract." Two simple sentences—the exchange of "can't" for "won't"—broke the conspiracy of silence that had ruled my day. Blotting my eyes with the heel of my hand, I left the treeless streets of campus behind.

"Theymadefunofmeforaskingaquestion." The day spewed from me in a solid stream, deep guttural breaths its only punctuation.

"I'm surprised you lasted the day," Augie said, after I described it. "I would've left after the uniform bullshit."

"I kept hoping it would get better." I opened my window and inhaled newly-mowed grass. "And they didn't give us that contract

190 • ONE BAD MOTHER

until the end." Suburban pools and single-family homes replaced the plastic lawn furniture and astroturf of the city. The farther away from the academy I was, the more I could breathe.

Outside the Abington Friends School playground, the happy screams of children, still full of summer sunshine, washed over me.

"Can I call you later?"

I stripped off my polyester blue uniform, buttons popping while Gus and Grace galloped through rope tunnels, more comfortable on four legs than two. This, here, was an impossible transition: police academy to Quaker Lower School.

"Mommy!" They raced over, forgetting their game.

"How was it?" Gus wrapped himself around my leg in a giant panda hug.

"Not so good."

"Here, Mommy. Treasure." Grace handed me the first red leaves of fall.

"Were the police mean?" Gus asked.

"There was a lot of yelling." I fingered the filigreed edges of the leaves.

"Those are for you." With a poke, Grace brought me back to a world where a special rock or leaf could solve everything.

"Oh, thanks."

"You're welcome." The bangs she'd recently cut herself rose from her forehead in every direction, making her more angry crested chicken than serious young girl.

"The police are jackasses." Gus kicked a pile of woodchips. "How do they expect you to stay if they're mean to you?"

"Well," I struggled to explain to Gus what I didn't understand myself. "I don't think they're jackasses. And stop swearing. Don't think I didn't notice." I waggled a finger at him. "The police believe what they're doing is right."

"It's not, Mommy," Gus said. "It's not. They made you cry." I nodded. Sometimes the logic of eight-year-olds made perfect sense.

"When are you going to stop crying, Mom?" Gus slammed his foot into the pile again.

"Probably not for a while."

"We don't like to see you sad," Grace told me.

"I know, but it's a weird kind of happy-sad." I pulled them close. After the air conditioning of the academy, their bodies were warm, alive.

"The police are assholes," Grace repeated.

"If you two don't stop swearing," I said, holding them away from me in warning, "I'm going to call 9-1-1."

"Fine." Grace raised a hand, always ready to threaten the world with an invisible hammer. "Do it. I have some things I want to say to them, right now."

"Let's go home." I pulled Grace's hand, steering us back toward the ordinary, to the daily rituals of homework, dinner, baths, and bedtime stories.

That evening, I called the academy's emergency number. No one answered. At 6 a.m., I tried again. "Don't call in absent on a snow day," Sergeant Sparkplug had warned. "The person who picks up the phone at six in the morning isn't going to be very under-standing since he managed to drag his sorry ass to work when you couldn't be bothered." It must've been snowing pretty hard on September 16th in Northeast Philadelphia because no one answered the phone until 8:30 a.m.

"I'm calling to withdraw," I told the desk officer.

"Can I ask why?" His question floated, disembodied, far away from my warm kitchen.

"Well, I can't be there at seven," I squirted Lysol onto a sponge. A late-for-the-bus-whirlwind had raged through my kitchen, leaving full glasses of orange juice and smears of strawberry jam behind. "You told me to be there at eight—"

"We don't really mean seven," he said, his voice measured and kind. "It's just a suggestion. Roll call is at eight. We can work this out. They're doing roll call now. Why don't I have the lieutenant call you after?"

"There's one more thing." I flicked a soggy Cheerio into the sink. "I can't sign that three-year contract."

"I don't know anything about a three-year contract."

"The last page of the packet says we have to pay back our salary if we don't work for the city for two consecutive years."

"Oh, that." He brushed my objections aside. "I don't think that's even legal. To my knowledge, we've never enforced that contract. It's there so candidates don't get poached by other departments after we pay to train you."

"I get it." Standing my ground was easy with coffee reheating, surrounded by the familiar smell of clean. "It's your standard non-compete clause. I still don't want to sign it."

"We can work this out," the desk officer repeated. "Why don't I have Lieutenant McPatrick call you."

The lieutenant called me two times that morning. I didn't pick up. Instead, I ran. Leaves dappled the path. A few pumpkins sat on front stoops. The season was changing, not pausing for my disappointment. Every few strides, the thought of returning to the academy surfaced, only to be squashed by the nauseas of memory. Emptied, at the end of ten miles, I turned homeward to make the call.

"No harm, no foul. This isn't for everyone," the lieutenant said. Maybe he heard the steel in my voice, the growing seeds of my disgust, or maybe forty-something housewives were disposable. Whatever it was, he didn't try to persuade me to stay.

"I'm just too old for this." In the face of his silence, I couldn't stop talking. "I don't need to be told not to go out and get drunk or get in a bar fight—"

"We've had people your age come through before. Just last class I had a forty-six-year-old woman graduate. She's going to make a great cop. But you need to come in to resign. We'll show you how to write this in a memo."

"Can't I just fax or email my withdrawal?"

"No." On this he was definite. "It looks better for you if you come in. The captain will want to interview you. Come in when you can." Apparently, all you had to do to get the police department to treat you like a human being was to quit.

That afternoon, I sat in my study and drafted my memo. On the street below, a flatbed truck unloaded mowers and blowers with a clang. I would not be schooled by the academy on how to write. At my desk, I could reclaim all the voices the PPD had stolen. A memo might not be extraordinary, but this I could do. Without multiple exclamation points.

MEMORANDUM
DATE: 09-16-16
TO: Lt. John McPatrick #381, Recruit Training Section
FROM: Megan Williams, Police Recruit Officer
SUBJECT: **RESIGNATION**

Please accept my resignation from the Philadelphia Police Academy, effective immediately, for the following reasons:

1. Although I greatly looked forward to working for the Police Department after graduation, I am unwilling to sign the "CERTIFICATE OF AGREEMENT" which requires that I reimburse the City of Philadelphia, in full, for my compensation and benefits received while at the Police Academy if I do not "remain in active employment by the Philadelphia Police Department for a continuous period of two years immediately following the initial certification." When added to the eight months spent at this Academy, this amounts to a thirty-two-month contract, without the guarantee of employment in return or even the knowledge of what the two-year position might be. I am unable to embrace the uncertainty and one-sidedness of this Agreement.

I could have stopped there. I knew I probably should. Leaf blowers circled my neighbor's house, the sound fading and approaching in waves. A mower coughed to life, filling my office with the sweet smell of benzene. *I love the smell of napalm in the morning.* I continued typing.

2.   While I was fully committed to the 8-4 workday, I cannot work in a workplace that employs the gender-discriminating policy of "no excuses for childcare issues." As a college professor and elite running coach, I have never missed a day or been late to work. However, as the mother of twins who were born prematurely at 29 weeks, I also realize that *LIFE HAPPENS* when you have children, even when you implement a "second, third, and fourth back-up plan." On Monday morning, for example, the City of Philadelphia school bus was supposed to pick my children up at 6:55; it never came. As a result, I had to drive them to school in Jenkintown, where early-care begins at 7:30. The early-care provider was five minutes late, which gave me twenty-five minutes to get to the Academy on-time. Which I was. As any responsible adult realizes, however, had there been an accident on the road or a snow day at school, the result might have been different, and I would have been punished with sit-ups, demerits, or the threat of expulsion. To me, this lateness is not the same as an eighteen-year-old who sleeps in because he drank too much the night before. The Philadelphia Police Academy, however, treats the two as equal, and I cannot serve an employer who threatens to punish me for taking care of my children and treats "childcare issues" or "Little Jimmy getting the sniffles" as a sign of personal failing and weakness.

Reading my words, I realized just how much the PPD had set me up to fail. Unlike friends who attended medical school for a second career and were put in a group of "non-traditional students," the academy grouped everyone together. Prior to training, all candidates were equally worthless. Age, experience, and education held no value. To separate candidates would be to coddle, to offer special treatment. Not once during the application process had the department suggested I talk to another woman about what were largely childcare issues. "Little Jimmy" might loom large in my self-conception, snot and all, but he was only ever an aside to the PPD.[8]

Hands on my keyboard, I paused. After reading my letter, the PPD would think I was an entitled and over-educated woman. So be it. Sometimes writing needed to be about more than your intended audience. Fragments of Spanish drifted through the open window. Beneath the piles of leaves, the grass emerged an electric green, uncertain if it was fall or spring, if it was supposed to grow or die. I had one more point to make:

3. Equally important was my overwhelmingly negative reaction to the "Shock and Awe" intimidation tactics employed by the Police Academy. While I understand that the Philadelphia Police Department fancies itself a paramilitary organization, in its first introduction to recruits no attempt was made to balance these concomitant bullying tactics with

---

[8] Only 12 percent of sworn officers and 3 percent of police leadership in the United States are women. Other English-speaking countries have nearly twice these percentages (Karen Tumulty, "One simple fix for our broken policing system: Hiring more women" (*Washington Post* 21 September 2023). Citing research that female officers use less force and see better outcomes, the 30 x 30 Initiative was created with the goal "to increase the representation of women in police recruit classes to 30% by 2030, and to ensure police policies and culture intentionally support the success of qualified women officers throughout their careers" (30 x 30 initiative.org). Under the leadership of Police Commissioner Danielle Outlaw, in March of 2021, the Philadelphia Police Department signed this pledge ("Philly Police pledges at least 30% of its incoming officers will be women by 2030" (*PhillyVoice* 27 March 2021)..

a mention of "community service" or the role of the Police Department to "protect and serve." I remain bitterly disappointed—one might even say "shocked"—by the complete and marked omission of these qualities, as I initially wanted to join the Police Department to give back to and serve the community where I have lived for thirty years.

Police Recruit Signature
Megan Williams, PhD

I can't say that I didn't feel sad, that my throat wasn't a little bit raw, when I drove down Comly Road to deliver my letter. Each time I replayed that first day, it hurt, a hardened cuticle I couldn't cut to the quick. Still, I kept returning, trying to worry it free, to find some small doubt I could hold onto that would allow me to return to the academy. It was only one day. Maybe it would get better. Maybe I was overly sensitive. A 1200-meter dash in a polyester uniform carrying forty pounds of books wasn't such a bad way to start a morning. So what if I got yelled at? I was tough enough.

A sea of blue uniforms undulated on the plaza outside the academy, its parts indistinguishable in the shimmering morning. I pulled next to the "Reality-Based Training" building, whatever that was. Preferential parking was one of the perks of resigning. The cars of the older recruits were cool to the touch. Their day had begun hours ago. Janai, Lupe, Blondie, the Crewcut Twins. They were all there. I scooched down, my head barely visible, a parody of a bad stakeout.

Yeah, no. I wasn't doing this. I kept driving. I wasn't going to walk the gauntlet past my former classmates to quit. I would go to Starbucks until the lunch truck left.

I knew all the insults. *She wasn't hard-core. Couldn't hack it. Just a middle-aged mom. This is the police academy. What did she expect, a liberal arts seminar?* They weren't much different from the voices in my head. The horrible sense of being unmoored ebbed and flowed through my days, never far from the surface. I was angry at myself for being so naive. Furious at the police academy. At the bottom of everything was grief, the bedrock into which all the feelings over lost opportunities and freedoms drained.

"What did you expect?" friends said. "It's the Philadelphia Police."

"I thought it was getting better." To them, I was a wide-eyed ten-year-old, complaining about how unfair my world was. My privileged background had made me an optimist. For all my cynicism, I believed in humanism—that we, as a people, had the ability to learn from our mistakes. I'd started this process with nothing but respect for the police. Now, when I was on errands with my kids and saw a police officer, I was scared. Terrified of what it meant to be an officer, to have let all the rules and prejudices of the academy seep into your soul.

"Couldn't you stay at least another week?" friends asked, disappointed. For the past two years, I'd been a great cocktail story.

Outside Starbucks, a Money Access Machine lay discarded in an office park, emptied of cash, its rainbow markings forever unlit. Northeast Philadelphia, like the Philadelphia Police Department, was a relic of another time. Or maybe that was just me. I didn't know it then, but it would take more days than I could count before I stopped envisioning what the recruits of Class #381 were doing, tracing their activities in my mind as if they were a skeleton-me, a phantom of what could have been. Every morning when I sat down at my computer to write, they were there, getting dressed, hurrying to roll call, sprinting onto campus with bags flying. May 26, 2017, would have been my graduation date.

Now it became the day I hoped my ghost-life would end.

What happened? Detective Brody emailed me when he received the revised class list. I considered not responding. Then I remembered that after two years, he, too, was invested in my application. I forwarded him my memo with a brief explanation. We never spoke again.

Two chalky Starbucks hot chocolates later, I returned to campus. In the academy lobby, the desk officer stopped me.

"Where're you going?" She scratched her head, bewildered by my civilian attire.

"Room 211."

"For what?"

"To resign."

"Okay." She turned away, embarrassed.

"Do you want me to sign in?" I pointed to the book in front of her.

"Oh, right. I should probably have you do that."

I signed and climbed the floating staircase that had greeted me in 2015. On that blustery November day, I'd been too intimidated by the shouting to notice the dress code signs. *#3. No Shorts.* Super.

"What should I wear?" I'd agonized over breakfast that morning.

"I don't think it really matters, hon," Augie said, his voice full of Cheerios and irony. "You're quitting." For the second time, my Boston Marathon T-shirt and spandex shorts made an appearance at the academy. Sometimes life did come full circle, even if you returned to the beginning changed.

The connected hallways on the second floor were silent, flanked by classrooms filled with computers and students. There was no Room 211. Years of Rocky Alpha Force Zippers had scuffed the lines off the linoleum floor tiles. This could have been any university building during exam week. Calm and ordinary, the hallways mocked me. I kept walking. There was still no Room 211. A sign read, *MAKE THE RIGHT CHOICES.*

I pushed open the door.

"I'm here to resign," I said to a room full of office cubicles. From the outside looking in, the academy was relaxed, unexceptional. This was an office like any other. The walls were covered with block lettered cards and crayon pictures—*I love you Daddy* and *You are the best Mommy Ever!!*

"So it wasn't for you, huh?" The officer closest to me stood, as if in sympathy.

"Nope." In a nearby cubicle, the older Eastern European sergeant spoke into the phone. Lieutenant Lurch craned his long neck around a carpeted divider. "Sir, here's my memo." I handed him the paper.

He scanned it and then my face. "I'll go down and give this to the captain. He's probably going to want to talk to you."

"Have a seat," the officer offered.

"No, thanks."

"No, no, no," Sergeant Iron Curtain said into her phone. "Those permits were for the last class. We have a new class that came in on Monday." She sat a little straighter, proud of this, her personal accomplishment. "Ninety new students."

Make that eighty-nine.

"Better you should find out now than later," the officer said.

"True." Textbooks sat on the floor, their titles printed in gilded letters. *Law Enforcement in Pennsylvania, Vol. II.* One of the many books I'd never read. *Join the Philadelphia Police: Make a Difference* the poster said. It no longer filled me with pride and want. *The police department doesn't need to change.*

As if conjured by the mere memory of his voice, Lieutenant Lurch materialized.

"Williams," he said. "You're good to go. But one last thing." He faced me, tone suspiciously personable. "All you have to do now is go down to Eighth and Race and do your paperwork."

"Paperwork?"

"Exit paperwork," he smiled.

Never had a job been so hard to quit. I was not driving to the Roundhouse. The police had copy machines. Access to the postal service. They could shuttle my memo back and forth between the lot of them. I was done. For two years, I'd jumped when they said jump. They no longer owned my ass.

"Oh, I forgot." I handed him a five-dollar bill. "Can you give this to Lopez? I don't know his first name. I had to borrow it to pay my union dues."

"You don't need those anymore." He waved me toward the door.

"I know. But he deserves it back."

"Sure." He took my money, then asked, "Do you know how to get to the Roundhouse?"

"On my way there right now." My last communication with the department was a deliberate lie. I jogged down the hallway and collided with Sergeant Sparkplug.

"Hello," he said, looking at my bare legs. Clearly he had no memory of me as a recruit. I was, after all, his age. We were both attractive forty-somethings. Part of my class, divided into platoons, trailed behind him. Lupe, Janai, Acne Boy, and Hittin' It. In the place of sadness or shame, I felt maternal. Mother Ginger in the Nutcracker. I wanted to draw the candidates to me, to encircle them. They needed to know that being tough enough didn't always mean bowing your head and soldiering on.

Sometimes it meant holding onto what you most valued—putting "Little Jimmy," Gus and Grace, even your own voice first. Sometimes it meant that the things other people said made you weak—children, therapy, age—were the very things that made you strong. The academy had tried to take these from me, but now I would grasp them in my hands, write their very ordinariness across the page.

Facing my former classmates, I realized I had to write again with hope—the hope that someday, someone would read my words about this experience. If I were very lucky, that someone would see herself here. To that reader, trapped in one of the many ordinary tragedies that define motherhood or life itself, the story of a woman who wanted to become a police officer because her daughter put a hammer through a wall would make perfect sense. She would understand the desire to get out of the fucking house. She would recognize that what was extraordinary was not the story itself that she was reading, but the fact that it was shared.

"Make way! Make way!" A clean-cut recruit shouted and pointed at me. One hand on the railing, I paused. Maybe I looked as if I had some authority, or maybe he was just playing it safe, covering his bases in case I was a super-sleuth undercover cop. The recruits flattened themselves awkwardly against the banister.

"Oh," I said. "You don't need to 'make way.' It's just me."

Enjoy more about

One Bad Mother

Meet the Author

Check out author appearances

Explore special features

ABOUT THE AUTHOR

Previous to her decision to apply to the police department, **Megan Williams** was a professor of English at various universities for over twenty years. After graduating from Haverford College, Megan received her Ph.D. in English from Temple University and taught at Lafayette College and Santa Clara University. Portions of One Bad Mother have received recognition from the New Millennium Award in Nonfiction, the Cagibi Magazine Prize, Panther Creek Award in Non-Fiction, and William Faulkner Creative Writers' Competition. Last year, Williams won the PNWA award for nonfiction. She and her family currently reside in Bellingham, Washington.

ACKNOWLEDGMENTS

Many thanks go into the writing of a book. Not to mention quite a few screw yous as well.

In the journey that has been this book, which is, in essence, a journey about being seen—both by other people and by myself, the most hurtful comments have been those that have erased me. I have reprinted some of these for posterity in the hope that they will encourage other writers to keep going:

This book would be better if you took the stuff about being a mother out.

Me: Like taking Russia out of Anna Karenina?

Exactly.

This book would be better if you were Black.

This book would be better if you had become a police officer.

Moving on to the more important thanks:

To my sister Tamsen for always taking my calls and giving me a reality check about motherhood. Yes, being pregnant feels like the world's worst hangover. Without the bonus. I only wish you had been able to keep your kids from screaming when we talked. I always could.

To Rachel Clarke for the support and the snark. It is always good to be reminded that some of the people from one's high school years remain jerks.

To Dona Templeman for talking me off a ledge when I was pregnant and for every Wednesday since.

To the NICU nurses at UCSF for loving my babies and for teaching me not to worry. Which might have only been partially successful.

To Oliver Radclyffe for *Frighten the Horses*, which renewed my faith and interest in writing, and for your suggestion that I really needed to put more blood and gore into my hospital scenes.

To Gladys for telling me to shut up and write.

To Mr. Nelson who taught us to pay attention to tone in 9th grade, and who suggested I try to be the person I was on paper in real life.

To Barbara for always having a spare room and time to listen.

To Jeanne Calloway who tirelessly read a chapter a week and kept me on a schedule, all while teaching Lower School. You literally could not pay me enough.

To Ann B.B. and the AFS book club and Susan Arteaga for reminding me when I most needed it that people still love a good story.

To my cohort at The Writer's Hotel—particularly Carol Smith, Margaret Lee, Jody Ulate, Julie Lambert, David Gibson, and Lisa Ellison, our fearless leader aka the woman we would all follow out of an airplane while listening to heavy metal.

To Nana. You have been my editor since I learned to read. These many years later, you are still the best line editor I know. And your voice is stuck in my head forever. Thank you for your endless support during all the years that neither of us thought this manuscript would ever see the light of day.

To Barclay for always being ready to go for a run to talk about a piece I sent you at the last minute. You are a genius at distilling my writing down to what I really mean. You are my ideal reader. Can I send you my next chapter? But first, can you tell me why, if Barbie can do it all, she doesn't have children?

To Karen for making "the world's best wheel pasta" and for teaching me how to hug.

To Rachel Salzman for sharing the topography of childhood and for asking when I was going to get this manuscript out into the world.

To my running group—the Megans, Christine, Nancy, and Cheryl. The Hot Mamas. You kept me going more times than you know.

To my horse friends for giving me space to breathe. And for taking care of my third child.

To GBRC and the Wednesday night running crew for planning a party a year in advance and for listening to my hypoxic ramblings.

To Cheryl for reading this with a three-day old baby. Enough said.

To the Impalas for teaching me that the only thing better than long runs with friends is long runs with friends who read.

To Nancy Y. I'm sorry I rolled my eyes the first time you came to practice. You showed me good.

To Kristi Beck for teaching me that sometimes the very best stories are the ones that don't get to be told.

To Augie for living this whole experience with me, including me reading it aloud to you during Friday night cocktail hour.

To Meghan with an H for teaching me how to calm the f*ck down.

To Julia and Vicki at Sibylline for taking a chance.

To Jack and Clara for taking the night shift and to the DeLucas for living in the NICU with us.

BOOK GROUP QUESTIONS

One Bad Mother
by Megan Williams

1. Change represents a major theme in this memoir—from the author's wish that she could reinvent herself like Gatsby to the police department's assertion that it "doesn't need to change." Do you think that the author is the same person at the beginning as she is at the end? How do you interpret the final line "it's just me"?

2. Throughout this book, Megan wants someone to ask her why she wants to become a police officer. Why do you think she applied to the academy and how do you think she would answer this question today?

3. Recent media coverage of the 30 x 30 Initiative has argued that many, if not most of the problems facing police departments, would be solved were more women in their ranks. From your experience, what do you think about this suggestion?

4. What does it mean to be a "Bad Mother" in this book, in your daily personal life, and in your culture as a whole? Why did Megan Williams choose this as her title?

5. The notion of "testing" runs through the book—as a parent and as a candidate. What do you think of the police department's criteria for "success" during this admissions process?

6. Much of the discussion after George Floyd's murder has focused on the need to radically revise the role the police play in the United States. After reading this memoir, did your perspective on the police change?

7.   *One Bad Mother* is a "braided memoir." The twin timelines of motherhood and police are combined to create a complex narrative. Of the two storylines, which did you find most important and compelling? Why do you think the author structured her book this way?

8.   In *Chapter Two: Running in Circles,* Megan tells her athlete "running should be about loving your body." She then immediately retracts this statement as a lie. How would you characterize the author's relationship to her body in this book? Does it change when she has children and applies to the academy?

Sibylline Press is proud to publish the brilliant work of women authors over 50. We are a woman-owned publishing company and, like our authors, represent women of a certain age.

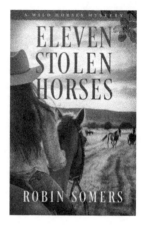

Eleven Stolen Horses:
A Wild Horses Mystery
BY ROBIN SOMERS

MYSTERY
Trade Paper, 306 pages (5.315 x 8.465) | $17
ISBN: 9781960573865
Also available as an ebook and audiobook

News reporter Eleanor Wooley wants
to start her life over in the foothills of
the Sierra Nevada but when her new
best friend suddenly disappears, she
finds herself in pursuit and in grave
danger instead.

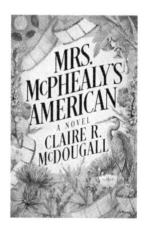

Mrs. McPhealy's American:
A Novel
BY CLAIRE R. McDOUGALL

FICTION
Trade Paper, 344 pages (5.315 x 8.465) | $19
ISBN: 9781960573865
Also available as an ebook and audiobook

A one-way ticket to his ancestral
home of Scotland lands beleaguered
Hollywood director Steve Mc-
Naught at his distant relative's, Mrs.
McPhealy's, in Locharbert where
he's an immediate outcast and soon
discovers that even love with a local
can't save him.

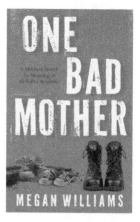

One Bad Mother: A Mother's Search for Meaning in the Police Academy
BY MEGAN WILLIAMS

MEMOIR
Trade Paper, 224 pages (5.315 x 8.465) | $17
ISBN: 9781960573858
Also available as an ebook and audiobook

A book for every mother who thinks she is failing the test of motherhood. Or thinks that challenging athletic feats or professional achievements may be easier than being a mother. That is—most of us. This is the thinking that landed the author in the police academy looking for win.

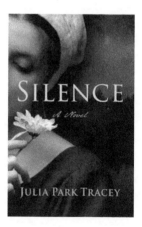

Silence: A Novel
BY JULIA PARK TRACEY

HISTORICAL FICTION
Trade Paper, 272 pages (5.315 x 8.465) | $18
ISBN: 9781736795491
Also available as an ebook and audiobook

A whiff of sulfur and witchcraft shadows this literary Puritan tale of loss and redemption, based on this best-selling historical fiction author's own ancestor, her seventh great-grandmother.

For more books from **Sibylline Press**, please visit our website at **sibyllinepress.com**

Printed in the USA
CPSIA information can be obtained
at www.ICGtesting.com
JSHW021233030824
67488JS00004B/7